Introduction

Still dripping wet from His baptism Jesus trudged along the muddy banks of the Jordan straight into the desert for a forty-day retreat into the wild. Why forty days? In the Bible, forty days is a time for change.

When God sent forty days of rain to flood the earth, it was a time of cleansing and regeneration. Both times Moses received the 10 Commandments he spent forty days on the mountain.

Elijah spent forty days of searching for God after the incident on Mt. Carmel. In the book of Jonah, God gave Ninevah forty days to change their wicked ways.

After His resurrection, Jesus spent forty days with His disciples preparing them for the work of the gospel before ascending into heaven.

The fact that Jesus went to the desert for forty days to prepare for ministry underlines the importance of being deliberate about change.

When I was in college my couch became a last resort to find spare change for much needed burritos. When money was tight I would lift up the cushions of the thirty-year-old sofa and hope to find change that accidentally slipped out from the pockets of guests. Clearly, there are better ways to save money. Likewise, there are better ways to acquire change.

While there is nothing magical about "forty days" it represents a season where actions can become habits. Michelle Joseph summarizes the process of habit formation: "Frequently repeated thoughts or actions create neural pathways and the more frequent the repetition, the stronger the connection and the wider the pathway will become." (Michelle Joseph, http://www.make-or-break-habits. com/how-habits-are-formed/) When it comes to spiritual growth, forty days of intentional spiritual exercise will begin to produce unmistakable change in our life.

The most basic element to spiritual growth is not only the belief that we can grow but the expectation that we are created to grow. Jesus made some bold claims about the change that would occur in His disciples:

"You did not choose me, but I chose you and appointed you to go and bear fruit-fruit that will last." (John 15:16 [NIV])

"The student is not above the teacher, but everyone who is fully trained will be like their teacher." (Luke 6:40 [NIV])

"Very truly I tell you, whoever believes in me will do the works I have been doing, and they will do even greater things than these, because I am going to the Father." (John 14:12 [NIV])

We can change. We should transform. We are meant to grow.

Real change—true spiritual growth is the result of divine grace at work in our life. To experience this kind of change, we must get off our spiritual couch and give God access to our hearts by giving Him the time, the freedom, and the opportunity to abide in us.

[Forty Days Wild]

No one accidentally stumbles toward spiritual growth. The life change so many seek is both personal and intentional. Growth comes by exercise and exercise awakens the muscles of the soul to ache when we work them.

Defy boredom. Confront pride. Bow in humility. Speak up. Stay Quiet. Stretch the mind. Practice kindness. Exhaust resources. Resist the spotlight. Forgive generously. Launch out in faith. Remain still.

Know that getting off the couch is never comfortable, but just beyond your comfort zone is where growth begins. Are you ready?

Before you begin...

Know that *Forty Days Wild* is designed to practice the spiritual disciplines with a partner, mentor, or a small group. Partners or groups are recommended to hold us accountable and it is well known that we learn better when we learn together.

Participants read and practice the daily exercises individually and debrief with each other at least once a week in a group meeting. The following is a list of exercises we will practice for the next forty days.

- Prayer
- Confession
- Being Alone/Quiet
- Sacrifice

- Fellowship
- Service
- Fasting and Feasting
- Sabbath

- Bible Study
- Secret Goodness
- Worship
- Storytelling

At the beginning of each week there will be a short introduction providing background for the exercises to engage in.

 Each day begins with a snapshot from the life of Christ (His words or actions).

 Following the passage from the life of Christ will be a followed by a devotional thought to inspire and equip the participants to think and act.

 At the end of each daily thought there are suggested activities to challenge those who read to action. Into the Wild urges the participants to practice the spiritual disciplines purposefully and reflectively, and consistently.

At the end of each week there are questions for reflection and discussion that equip the participants to meet and share together from their experience during the week.

—WEEK 1—
Prayer and Guidance Through Scripture

Prayer

The spectrum of genuine prayer can range from the almost knee-jerk cry, "God, Help!" to a entire life walk with God as Enoch did. Consider some of the thoughts others have penned on the nature, work and experience of prayer:

Dallas Willard maintains that, "Prayer is conversing, communicating with God."[1]

Richard Foster states, "Prayer catapults us onto the frontier of the spiritual life. Of all the spiritual disciplines prayer is the most central because it ushers us into perpetual communion with the Father...Prayer is the central avenue God uses to transform us."[2]

E. M. Bounds says "What the church needs today is not more machinery or better, not new organizations or more novel methods, but men whom the Spirit of God can use men of prayer, men mighty in prayer."[3]

One of the goals this week is to deliberately enter into conversation with God. Paul urges believers to "Devote yourselves to prayer, being watchful and thankful." (Colossians 4:2) In the same way that new conversations sometimes begin slowly and warm up with time, praying may begin awkwardly but with time the interaction becomes more meaningful and free. Beware of the tendency some have to learn all about prayer but avoid actually praying.

While prayer is a priority of the spiritual life, learning to know God and do His will for your life is the natural "next step" or exercise on this journey.

Guidance Through Scripture

One of my favorite book titles is, The Bush Won't Burn and I'm All Out of Matches by Daniel Schaeffer. The title depicts a desperate struggle to prompt God to speak, and speak now. Imagine Moses hopping around the desert lighting bush fires whenever he had a question or needed guidance. God's communication through a burning bush arrested Moses to pay attention to God. The Book of Hebrews comments on the ancient process of revelation, stating:

"In the past God spoke to our ancestors through the prophets at many times and in various ways, but in these last days he has spoken to us by his Son..." (Hebrews 1:1,2)

God's communication is meant to guide us to know Him. Jon Dybdahl urges:

"We must have a holy purpose in place for study to be truly in a spiritual sense. Intellectual curiosity has nothing inherently wrong with it. A desire for facts is not evil. But study as a spiritual discipline must move far beyond mere curiosity and intellectual knowledge. The more we have fixed in our minds a desire to know God and His will for our lives, the more spiritually productive our study becomes."[4]

For centuries the western world believed that since the Bible is true the truths therein are binding and relevant. In the last century the cultural mood has shifted these assumptions to value what is powerful over what is true. "What works" is perceived as more important than "what is right." What is "doable" seems to be more valuable than what God "declares." The end result is that unless our encounter with the Bible is experiential, it is unnecessary. What may be surprising is that Jesus fosters the idea that God's word is to be incarnated into our lives with purpose before it can be meaningful for us in an enduring way:

"Therefore everyone who hears these words of mine and puts them into practice is like a wise man who built his house on the rock." (Matthew 7:24)

"If anyone chooses to do God's will, he will find out whether my teaching comes from God or whether I speak on my own." (John 7:17)

"He guides the humble in what is right and teaches them his way." (Psalm 25:9)

"But whoever lives by the truth comes into the light, so that it may be seen plainly that what he has done has been done through God." (John 3:20)

As we journey through the pages of Scripture and practice the work of reading reflectively, meditating, scouring and scratching at timeless truths, good authority assures that we will "taste and see that the LORD is good." (Psalm 34:8)

Dallas Willard shows the relationship between Bible study and some of the other activities of the spiritual life:

"In study we also strive to see the Word of God at work in the lives of others, in the church, in history, and in nature...We not only read and hear and inquire, but we meditate on what comes before us; that is, we withdraw into silence where we prayerfully and steadily focus upon it. In this way its' meaning for us can emerge and form us as God works in it the depths of our heart, mind and soul."[5]

Think of prayer and Bible study as a dialogue with God about you and Him. Enter into the conversation with humility and a willingness to hear and obey God's voice.

DAY 1 · CLOSE THE DOOR

"And when you pray, do not be like the hypocrites, for they love to pray standing in the synagogues and on the street corners to be seen by men. I tell you the truth, they have received their reward in full. But when you pray, go into your room, close the door and pray to your Father, who is unseen. Then your Father, who sees what is done in secret, will reward you." (Matthew 6:5-13)

Do people really try to be seen praying? If anything, the current trend is to keep religion private. The advice from Jesus on prayer is simply, "go into your room, close the door and pray to your father."

Close the door. Closing the door requires courage. Even though you close the door to pray, the clock still ticks. A list of "things to do today" scratches like a hungry cat at the pantry door. Even when everything seems to be in order, you may still simmer with unrest at the nagging suspicion that you are leaving something out. But close the door. Tell the world, the patients, the clients, the customers, your teacher, your parents or children not to interrupt you because you have an appointment—kind of a grown up "time out."

Today's passage is not about praying in public but about the object of prayer. The focus is on who you pray to.

Sitting in a booth at a restaurant, I overheard the conversation of the couple behind me. It was obviously a first date. The "newby" in the booth behind me couldn't stop talking about himself. I never once heard the voice of his date. Rookie mistake. You demonstrate you are interested in someone by listening attentively. Mark it down men! The way to a woman's heart may be nothing you say but how well you listen. The same might be true with prayer.

"Prayer is the opening of the heart to God as to a friend. Not that it is necessary, in order to make known to God what we are, but in order to enable us to receive Him. Prayer does not bring God down to us, but brings us up to Him."[6]

Close the door. For prayer to be powerful, it is imperative for you to close the door and enter into an honest conversation where God has your full attention. Have you ever prayed without thinking about God? It's not uncommon to say the words of a prayer and ignore the One to whom you pray.

As a teenager I learned a little of what it means to close the door and face God with no distractions. I helped in the sound booth at the back of the church so during the celebration of the Lord's Supper, the deacons who passed out the bread and the cup often overlooked me.

"Is this the way the church feels about young people?" I stewed, "Week after week I serve and no grape juice! What a sham!" I continued to simmer.

After the service, on my way to hang out with my friends, the pastor grabbed me and said, "Come with me." He clutched my hand in his and was pulling me through the crowd.

"What did I do?" I thought. My heart raced. I was too scared to ask. He opened the door to his office, ushered me in to a chair and went back to the door and locked it. Gulp! The lock clicked with deafening finality, just like in the movies. I almost began a premature confession, "I'm sorry about what I wrote in the church hymnal..." when he leaned over his desk and said, "I'm so sorry Troy. I know the deacon passed you again at communion and I don't want you to miss out on the experience." He reached back to the little black boxes behind his desk that held what I called "Communion in a box." Pastor White went through the whole service with me that day (including his sermon) and administered the Lord's Supper right there on his desk.

Awkward? Yes. But I looked over at the locked door and I knew that for that moment, I was the only member of his church. I was the only one that mattered. I had his full attention and he had mine.

Jesus says, "Close the door." Prayer is not about the time, words, posture or the way that you pray; it's more about meeting face to face the One you pray to. Does He have your full attention? What are the doors you need to close as you make time to encounter God?

 Find a place to pray where you deliberately go on the other side of a door and actually shut the door to be alone to pray. As you pray today, talk to God about the difficulties and joys you have found in moments of prayer. Imagine what God is doing while you pray.

When you pray, pray out loud. Name the distractions out loud to God in prayer.

Take a moment to think about what is on your mind and in your heart, going on in your life.

Make a list of the things you want to talk about with God before you pray.

Sing a song that focuses your heart and mind on the One you are praying to.

Reflect on the struggle of giving God your full attention in prayer. Why is that difficult? What works best for you? How do you think this will help you deepen your relationship with Jesus in the future?

DAY 2 · PRAYER WORKS

 "Again, I tell you that if two of you on earth agree about anything you ask for, it will be done for you by my Father in heaven. For where two or three come together in my name, there am I with them." (Matthew 18:19-20)

 The Washington Post reported, "more than half of Americans polled pray at least once a day." Although people tend to be diverse in their beliefs many still believe in prayer. Nevertheless, finding someone convicted by the absolute necessity of prayer is a bit rare. The story is told of a father who was desperate for prayer.

"I was taking my usual morning walk when a garbage truck pulled up beside. I thought the driver was going to ask for directions. Instead he showed me a picture of a cute little five-year-old boy. "This is my grandson, Jeremiah," he said. "He's on a life–support system at a Phoenix hospital." Thinking he would next ask for a contribution to his hospital bills, I reached for my wallet. But he wanted something more valuable than money. He said, "I'm asking everybody I can to say a prayer for him. Would you say one for him, please?"[7]

What a rush of joy it is to witness someone who believes in prayer so confidently and completely. In reality, it is more common to find those who wrestle with the belief in the power of prayer. To pray or not pray is not always the question. Even those who profess to "not believe" will pray if the situation they face forces them to wonder if there is something greater "out there." Many have asked thoughtful questions about prayer:

"Does God really hear my prayers?"

"Is God's mind already made up?"

"Do I have to pray constantly, more fervently, more faithfully?"

"Does prayer change me or the situation?"

"Do I ask according to His will, mine, or both?"

"Should I beg or even barter a deal?"

"Does yesterday's sin disqualify today's prayer request?"

"How much faith is a mustard seed—in terms I can measure?"

"Does God still heal?"

However you phrase the question, the bottom line is still—Does prayer work? James 5:16 claims that "The prayer of a righteous person is powerful and effective." Prayer is "powerful and effective" in at least two ways:

1. Prayer works on the one who prays.

2. Prayer works on the One to whom you pray.

People change when they pray. Let the skeptics denounce that as foolish—but if you really need proof, ask the people who pray. The mental, emotional and physical exercise of asking for help has the power to transform the one who prays. Look at some examples:

In my anguish I cried to the LORD, and he answered by setting me free. (Psalm 118:5)

When I called, you answered me; you made me bold and stouthearted. (Psalm 138:3)

Ask and you will receive, and your joy will be complete. (John 16:24)

Prayer clearly works on the one who prays. It's not magical—it's relational. Praying not only changes the one who prays, but prayer works on the Person to whom you pray.

Here are some examples of how prayer moved God to action.

Jabez cried out to the God of Israel, "Oh, that you would bless me and enlarge my territory! Let your hand be with me, and keep me from harm so that I will be free from pain." And God granted his request. (1 Chronicles 4:10)

The righteous cry out, and the LORD hears them; he delivers them from all their troubles. (Psalm 34:17)

When my life was ebbing away, I remembered you, LORD, and my prayer rose to you, to your holy temple...And the LORD commanded the fish, and it vomited Jonah onto dry land. (Jonah 2:7-10)

It gets better. Try this on for size: Prayer sometimes pushes God to change His mind. "Wait a minute," you say? Imagine the following scene.

God is infuriated at the children of Israel. God has delivered them from their oppressors and they were caught worshipping a golden calf saying, "The calf saved us!" What is God's response to their idolatry?

"I have seen these people," the LORD said to Moses, "and they are a stiff-necked people. Now leave me alone so that my anger may burn against them and that I may destroy them. Then I will make you into a great nation." (Exodus 32:9-10)

Moses prays:

"Why should the Egyptians say, "It was with evil intent that he brought them out, to kill them in the mountains and to wipe them off the face of the earth?" Turn from your fierce anger; relent and do not bring disaster on your people." (Exodus 32:12)

Is that legal? Can Moses do that? Where is the lightening bolt? Moses just crossed the line! He's gone too far! Everyone step away from the guy with the tablets of stone and the big stick, for he will soon be toast. Sorry. No fire from heaven that day. Look what did come down:

"Then the LORD relented and did not bring on his people the disaster he had threatened." (Exodus 32:14)

Manipulative? Maybe. Give the Father some credit. Maybe Moses knew God better than you and I. Maybe Moses knew about the soft spot in God's heart. Be shocked. Be appalled. But in the end, be grateful that the soft spot in the heart of God still beats warm for you and me. Is Moses' prayer manipulative? Perhaps his prayer is like a child coming to a Father pleading the desire of his heart. Label the prayer anyway you want, but you can't cut this story from Scripture, nor can you delete the many versus that describe God answering the prayers of people in active, tangible ways.

In the book The Great Controversy, Ellen White observes:

"Again, worldly wisdom teaches that prayer is not essential...Were not miracles wrought by Christ and His apostles? The same compassionate Saviour lives today, and He is as willing to listen to the prayer of faith as when He walked visibly among men. The natural cooperates with the supernatural. **It is a part of God's plan to grant us, in answer to the prayer of faith, that which He would not bestow did we not thus ask.**"[8]

Imagine the implications of the above statement. Are there things God is waiting to do for us if we would just ask? Clearly, what holds humanity back is not God's mysterious ways of working but the human hesitation to believe that God will answer. If the above is true, perhaps you might begin this journey by praying honestly and earnestly for God to work in your life in ways He would not if you chose not to pray.

Jesus said that "If two of you on earth agree about anything you ask for, it will be done for you by my Father in heaven." (Matthew 18:19)

The writer of Hebrews urges us to "...come boldly unto the throne of grace, that we may obtain mercy, and find grace to help in time of need." (Hebrews 4:16)

In the course of this day, seize the opportunity to pray boldly with someone. It could be your partner or someone less familiar—but venture into the presence of God with another person.

Rank your prayer life on the boldness scale:

[1]   [2]   [3]   [4]   [5]   [6]

Brazen & Bold   Subtle & Shy

What do you think God wants from your prayer life the most right now? What kinds of prayers seem to draw you closer to God and why do you think this is the case?

DAY 3 · THE WAR OF THE WILLS

Going a little farther, he fell to the ground and prayed that if possible the hour might pass from him. "Abba, Father," he said, "everything is possible for you. Take this cup from me. Yet not what I will, but what you will. (Mark 14:32-36)

William Dembski cited a prayer prayed by Homer Simpson that touches on what people pray for and whether they expect answers. Homer's wife tries to interrupt the prayer with news that she is pregnant with their third child:

Can't talk now—praying," he interrupts. "Dear Lord, the gods have been good to me and I am thankful. For the first time in my life everything is absolutely perfect the way it is. So here's the deal: you freeze everything as it is and I won't ask for anything more. If that is okay, please give me absolutely no sign. [pause] Okay, deal. In gratitude, I present to you this offering of cookies and milk. If you want me to eat them for you, please give me no sign. [pause] Thy will be done."[9]

While the ridiculous nature of this prayer may be obvious, the conflict between our personal desires and praying the words, "Thy will be done" is often subversive and dangerously subtle. The discussion about prayer and the will of God is among the trickiest, stickiest topics known to believers and skeptics alike. Arguably, young adults wonder about the dynamics between prayer and God's will because so much of their life is shaped by the decisions they make during this time. It is not uncommon for college students to get serious about God in light of the oncoming train of careers, relationships, marriage and family, etc. All of a sudden, it is not so crazy to wonder what God wants for their lives.

Most people who think about "God's will" may be tentative about praying for it because God may want something different, but for what we want. In the book Children's Letters to God, a child writes his prayer rather glibly, "Dear God, thanks for the baby brother, but what I asked for was a puppy."[10]

Honestly, one of the hardest prayers to pray is the prayer embracing what God wants for you instead of what you want. The story of Jesus praying in Gethsemane shows Christ to be tip-toeing the line between being human and divine. Even though He is able, Jesus is not kicking demons in the teeth. He's not re-creating the rotten flesh of a leprous man into baby-soft smoothness. The Son of God is not calling a child back from death to life or crafting word pictures that portray eternal truths. In the garden, Jesus is like us. He looks death in the face and doesn't want to taste it. His prayer is, "Is there any other way?"

Have you ever heard people use the phrase, "Lord willing"? For instance, "I'll plant the crops in the east field next year, Lord willing," or, "I'll see you at church on Wednesday, Lord willing." When we don't have control over the future it is not so hard to say, "Lord willing." It doesn't require much faith to hand over tomorrow promising, I'll be what you want me to be—I'll go where you want me to go—especially if it is what I'm planning to do anyway. What happens when the future is now and God's will is in direct conflict with your own? Did you hear the words Jesus spoke to His friends?

"My soul is overwhelmed with sorrow to the point of death. "

Notice He didn't say, "Who knows what tomorrow holds. I'm yours, Lord willing." He couldn't. Fortunately, Jesus knew the future.

Fortunately? He knew that the immediate future was an all-night brain bashing. He knew that morning light would bring the sentence of death. He knew that what tomorrow held for Him was a cross. Fortunately, He knew.

Can you imagine what a tragedy it would be if the crucifixion were an accident, a surprise? Calvary wouldn't be a sacrifice—it would be a tragic murder. Fortunately for us, He chose the cross; He chose the Father's will.

"The reason my Father loves me is that I lay down my life—only to take it up again. No one takes it from me, but I lay it down of my own accord. I have authority to lay it down and authority to take it up again. This command I received from my Father." (John 10:17-18)

When Jesus prayed, "Your will be done," He prayed with the full knowledge of God's plan for Christ's death. Believe me, the cross was only a small part of the pain Jesus feared. What made Jesus beg, "Let this cup pass from me" was the oncoming experience of Hell—God's condemnation of sin in Him.

"My God, My God, Why have you forsaken me?"

God's holy hatred of sin would be focused on the Sin Bearer. Who felt the love and glory of the Father more than the Son? The horror of God's absence promised to be even stronger for One who lived constantly in God's presence. Fortunately, Jesus chose for us the three biggest letters in the universe that split history with the same decisiveness as they split a sentence;

"Not my will, BUT Your will be done."

Why wouldn't you want His will for your life? Do you know something God doesn't? Is there a sense that you might be selling yourself short or missing out on something if you buy into His plan? Can you pray this prayer today—and mean it?

 What area of your life are you most afraid to surrender? Make a list of the top five things that tend to separate you from the Father and a list of the top five things that often bring you closer together. Talk to God honestly and openly about your lists. Be specific.

What song(s) come to mind when you think of praying/wanting God's will to be done in your life today? What are some of the words, and why do you think they speak to you?

DAY 4 · GETTING FORGIVENESS

And when you stand praying, if you hold anything against anyone, forgive him, so that your Father in heaven may forgive you your sins. (Mark 11:23-25)

What if there were a sin detector that reminded you of any issues between you and someone else before you prayed? If you harbored resentment in your heart, a beeper would sound at the beginning of your prayer as a reminder to make things right. A similar device was used in Thailand centuries ago to warn the guards at city gates of potentially dangerous people as they entered:

The gates were made of lodestone—a natural magnet. If a would-be assassin came in through the gate with a concealed dagger, the lodestone would pull at the hidden weapon like an invisible hand. Startled, the individual would involuntarily reach for the weapon. Trained guards, watching every movement, would then grab him.[11]

While there is no magic device that warns you when we something is "in the way," the notion of praying to God while harboring a rift between yourself and someone else is much like placing a dessert on a dirty plate.

I'm a once-a-year chef. I'm not proud of this title; I can cook, but mostly I don't. I like to save my moments of culinary genius for special occasions. One night, about fifteen high-school students came to my house for dinner. Originally, there were only supposed to be five, but teenagers develop a Velcro-like substance on their bodies, which causes them to stick together and multiply, especially when food is involved. I seized the moment for a vain display of my talents.

The meal: a brilliant pasta dish with steamed vegetables. The grand finale was an amazing sour cream lemon pie. The troupe devoured the meal as expected. When it came time for dessert, I was serving slices of pie when Jonathan presented his plate to me for a piece. I almost dropped the pie when I saw what was before me. It was horrible. Tomato sauce mixed with cheese. Salad dressing residue smeared callously around the plate. Crumbs from the garlic bread peppered everything. Broccoli specks littered the plate like confetti. My hand froze. I could not put that pie on his plate in that condition.

"What are you doing?" I bellowed.

Jonathan was surprised. "I'm getting some pie—what's your problem?"

"My problem?" I replied. "Your plate is a mess! I'm not putting this heavenly slice of ecstasy on that!"

I'm sure you can imagine his response when I made him clean his plate. But imagine how bad it would taste to mix leftover pasta with my beautiful pie. The true taste of the pie would never be experienced with the presence of garlic, tomato sauce and broccoli specks. So it is with the grace that comes through intimacy with God in prayer.

Jesus said, "And when you stand praying, if you hold anything against anyone, forgive him, so that your Father in heaven may forgive you your sins." (Mark 11:23-25)

Does that sound right? I thought forgiveness was free. I thought God's love had no strings attached. Unconditional love? Forgiveness sounds pretty conditional to me, but the context is more about effective prayers that do great things rather than your own personal forgiveness.

How can we engage the presence of God, throw ourselves at His mercy, and simultaneously hold resentment in our hearts toward someone else? Jesus asks his followers to treat undeserving people with the same mercy they receive from God on a regular basis. You don't deserve God's forgiveness any more than other people deserve yours.

Do you really want to be intimate with God? Do you want the free flow of His grace in your life? Then if grace comes down from heaven to you, so it must go from you to others.

When you pray, begin with a clean plate. Write the letter you need to write. Say the words you need to say. If you hold on to hatred or irritation, begin treating the hated person with grace. Grace won't taste like grace if you mix it with resentment.

"If I had cherished sin in my heart, the Lord would not have listened; but God has surely listened and heard my voice in prayer." (Psalms 66:18-19)

"If anyone turns a deaf ear to the law, even his prayers are detestable." (Proverbs 28:9)

"But your iniquities have separated you from your God; your sins have hidden his face from you, so that he will not hear." (Isaiah 59:2)

"When you ask, you do not receive; because you ask with wrong motives, that you may spend what you get on your pleasures." (James 4:3)

The question goes back to will. God's will is clear: Forgive abundantly, love unconditionally. Meet the needs of lost and lonely people with joy. Sacrifice and spend yourself as though that is the only meaningful thing in life. As you pray on this road, I have no doubt it will be wild—no end to the excitement, no end to the victories. Taste and see!

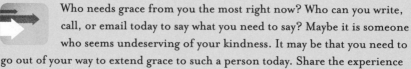

Who needs grace from you the most right now? Who can you write, call, or email today to say what you need to say? Maybe it is someone who seems undeserving of your kindness. It may be that you need to go out of your way to extend grace to such a person today. Share the experience with your partner or group.

Reflect on how this experience went today. What happened? How did it feel to take care of unfinished business before praying? What was the result? How can you continue to practice praying to God with a right spirit toward others?

DAY 5 · THE SOURCE AND SUBJECT

> You diligently study the Scriptures because you think that by them you possess eternal life. These are the Scriptures that testify about me, yet you refuse to come to me to have life. (John 5:39-43)

Leonard Sweet once asked, "How is it that we so easily get the point but miss the Person?" Jesus declares that the content of Scripture is about the Incarnate Son. Apparently, such a slight miscue of focus is easier than it might seem.

I was hiking in a state park and couldn't figure out which trail led back to the parking lot. I never claimed to have a keen sense of direction or any sense of direction for that matter. "Whoever made this map needs to take a walk in the wilderness before they try and make a map." I said the words out of frustration to a passerby in official looking outdoor clothing. What was I thinking?

The ranger in khaki shirt and forest green shorts just smiled tolerantly as she pointed to the trailhead junction that was only a hundred yards ahead. "That's the trail you want right up there." She pointed to another trail parallel to the one I was on, which I still maintain was impossible to see. Then, with a smile, she added, "Last year the rains washed out part of this area so we had to redirect the trial. When I made this map it was correct."

"Oh," I said out loud as I couldn't think of anything else to say to the "mapmaker." Being a multi-tasker, I became aware of my bad manners while I looked for a large rock crawl under or a cliff to jump off. Neither option was available. What were the odds of the map-maker being out and about for the daily patrol of the park at the very moment my mouth decided to open wide enough to say something stupid?

She initially seemed sympathetic to my embarrassment but chose to drive the point home, casually admitting, "It does seem a little confusing, but I have to admit, you are the first person to ask that question."

Touché. "It has to do with my sense of direction. I probably just didn't look at the map as carefully as I could have," I confessed.

"Up ahead, just past the creek," she said patiently.

I got out of there. Sometimes it's better to get away quickly than to linger around and find other ways to look foolish.

I thought about the encounter as I walked back to my car. If I were in trouble, would I trust the map or the ranger? Maps are printed, but people are personal. Trail maps are helpful, but trail guides are the real thing.

The map and the Map Maker. He is the reason for the Scriptures. The

Scriptures are about Him. The problem: We major in the map and minor in the Map-maker. It seems backwards. The Bible's primary purpose is to reveal a "Someone" to us. God's word offers us, not a paradigm or position, but a real, live, compassionate Savior. Without Jesus, the Book makes no sense and has no purpose, rhyme, or reason. The Bible is all about revelation—revealing the Son to all of creation.

Have you ever seen the 3-D pictures where there is an image hidden within another image? Sitting in the front seat of my car after shopping for groceries a picture on the back of a box of cereal caught my eye. The image was somewhat colorful, but a little fuzzy and obscure. I pulled out the box and read the instructions:

"In order to be able to see this picture, look directly into the picture and slowly bring the box closer to your face, then gradually pull it back. Keep your eyes directed at one spot on the box and the picture within the picture will emerge."

After several minutes attempting this ridiculous activity I looked at the minivan parked next to me and observed through my peripheral vision three kids laughing and pointing their fingers at me as I slowly drew the box to my nose—one last time. I never saw the picture.

Those of you reading this who easily see the image in 3D pictures are probably smiling a grin of self satisfaction. Well, enjoy it. I struggle with it, mainly because I'm trying to see the picture instead of allowing it to emerge. It takes time. Patience. Discipline. It takes focus and attention. In a similar way to 3-D pictures, so the Living Son of God emerges from the pages of the Bible. Notice what John (probably one of those guys who sees 3D images) says about the One who is The Word:

"The Word became flesh and made his dwelling among us. We have seen his glory, the glory of the One and Only, who came from the Father, full of grace and truth." (John 1:14)

How is God trying to speak to you today? Consider the travelers on the road on that Sunday two thousand years ago. Their world unraveled at Calvary. Their hopes were crushed when their Rabbi died. Their expectations and dreams were scattered along the trail as they walked away from Jerusalem.

They said all the right things to the traveler who mysteriously joined them on the road.

The disciples shared with Jesus (although they didn't recognize Him), "He was arrested, sentenced, killed, and rumors that we was alive the third day were going around." In a way, they packaged the gospel clearly in a few sentences. What were they thinking? What made their hearts burn? Jesus walked with them and explained it to them pointing out how the Bible prophesied that the Christ would suffer, die, and be raised up to life.

After some time, the walking, the sharing, and the struggling with this stranger saturated the hearts of these two believers and "click!" They saw Jesus.

The Bible says, "Then their eyes were opened and they recognized him, and he disappeared from their sight. They asked each other, "Were not our hearts burning within us while he talked with us on the road and opened the Scriptures to us?" (Luke 24:13-32)

The way God's Word gets into us has to do with the way we get into it. Think about the process of making a good cup of tea. If you put the bag in the hot water for a second or two, it only wets the bag but does not change the color or flavor at all. Let it sit longer. After a bit, a different color leaks out into the water and wisps of flavor swim in the cup before your very eyes. The longer the bag stays in the water, the more color and strength the flavor of the tea will have. I don't think it's much different with Bible study. Getting the point is easy—getting the Person takes time.

Study God's word to find the message He has for you. Invite the Holy Spirit to teach you throughout the day. Create a visual reminder of the passage that will cause you to reflect continually. Be patient. Allow the passage to sink in and then share what you have discovered with someone else. Reflect upon your experience with an in-depth approach to the Bible. Reflect on how Bible study is meaningful and effective for you.

Go to a bookstore or a library—even your own bookshelf—and find a biography that seems interesting to you. You don't have to read it, but look at the table of contents and ask yourself the following questions:

What does the table of contents tell me about this person?

To what degree will I be able to say that I know the person the book is written about?

If you had to describe the subject of this book to someone else, what would you be able to say from what you read?

How would you teach a third grader about the relationship between the purpose and Person of Scripture. The best way to learn anything is to consider how you might teach it.

Reflect on why knowing Christ through the Scriptures is difficult for you. Reflect on the moments when Jesus emerged like a 3-D image.

DAY 6 · IF THEY DON'T LISTEN

"But Abraham replied, 'Son, remember that in your lifetime you received your good things, while Lazarus received bad things, but now he is comforted here and you are in agony. And besides all this, between us and you a great chasm has been set in place, so that those who want to go from here to you cannot, nor can anyone cross over from there to us.' "He answered, 'Then I beg you, father, send Lazarus to my family, for I have five brothers. Let him warn them, so that they will not also come to this place of torment.' "Abraham replied, 'They have Moses and the Prophets; let them listen to them.' "'No, father Abraham,' he said, 'but if someone from the dead goes to them, they will repent.' "He said to him, 'If they do not listen to Moses and the Prophets, they will not be convinced even if someone rises from the dead.'" He said to him, "If they do not listen to Moses and the Prophets, they will not be convinced even if someone rises from the dead." (Luke 16:25-31)

How much does the miraculous really motivate? Does the sensation of some supernatural event ever change your life over the long haul? Think about it.

How long do stirring sermons on the second coming preoccupy your mind with expectant thoughts of heaven? The sermon stirs, but it does not secure your attention for much longer than a day or two.

Miraculous events bring us to our knees in thankful gratitude. An answered prayer. God is good. A healing. Jesus saves! The right job. The opened window or the closed door. The obvious and undeniable sensation that God is real—right now. Supernatural interruptions do inspire, but for how long?

What about the moments where you have been used by God—a word, a prayer, or an act of service that made a difference for someone else. The "spiritual high" of the Christian experience, the moment where God is real becomes just that: a moment. It has a beginning— and an end.

Jesus told the parable of the rich man and Lazarus to remind His listeners that acts of grace on earth are priceless and have eternal influence. The rich man had the chance to be compassionate to the beggar while they were both alive. Instead, they both died; the rich man went to hell while the beggar went to heaven. While the rich man was in hell, he was able to see the beggar resting comfortably in heaven. The rich man becomes determined to get the word back to his family about the how bad hell is. The rich man appeals to Abraham to send Lazarus, the beggar, back from the afterlife to warn his family. Abraham refuses to send someone from the dead to say what has already been revealed in Scripture. This is a parable using a fairy-tale-like legend to make a point. Please, don't get confused by your ideas about life after death and miss the two punch lines of the passage.

PUNCH LINE # 1

Your opportunity to live a life of compassion is today, not tomorrow and certainly not in the hereafter.

PUNCH LINE #2

Miracles and mystical phenomenon never replace God's Word. This principle grows out of the rich man's plea to Abraham when he begs, "Send Lazarus to warn my father and brothers of this place…"

Abraham answers, "They have Moses and the prophets, let them listen to them. Moses and the prophets are enough."

The reply? The rich man doesn't buy it. "If someone comes back from the dead, surely they will repent."

The answer and the lesson are clear: If they don't listen to Moses, they will not repent even if someone comes back from the dead."

There must be more! A sign? A miracle? Maybe just a feeling. "Yeah, that's it God—give me a feeling about what to do!"

Here is a question I have pondered lately: Jesus healed and helped tens of thousands of people directly during His ministry. How is it that less than twenty were there for Him in His final moments? What enduring impact do miracles have?

The whole experience of studying the Bible is a little less mysterious when you are aware of the Person behind the letter. It doesn't have to be a puzzle or some magical discovery.

Consider the young lady who entered my office brandishing a letter from her mother.

"My mother wrote me a letter and I want to talk with you about it. Do you have a second?" The way she said it clearly indicated that it might take more than a second.

"I can't believe she said this!" she said as she handed me the folded piece of notebook paper.

I fully expected some blistering judgmental diatribe but in the first few lines of the letter I sensed an honest appeal from a mother to passionately call her daughter to aim higher with her life. She was affirming but direct. Truthful yet unmistakably laced with hope and confidence in her daughter's capacity for doing what was right. The letter was touching, even compelling. I seized the moment to practice a bit of drama hoping the methodology would work.

"Unthinkable!" I snorted.

I continued to read but noticed she looked a bit surprised at my reaction.

"Un-be-lievable!" I pretended to be stunned.

"What?" she asked with a furrowed brow.

"I can't believe the audacity of a parent who would write this!" I continued.

"Really" she said a little tenuously.

"I mean, she is literally telling you that you're not living up to your potential! She is actually saying that your life is somehow misguided and not going in a good direction. That you are toying with a lifestyle that will eventually trap you! How dare she? How does she know what you are dealing with? Who does she think she is?"

"Well, she is my mother..." she began to defend her mom.

I replied indignantly, "I know, but what right does she have to say this stuff? I mean she does not sugar coat any of it. That's downright insensitive!" Luckily, my dramatic grand finale worked.

"She loves me. I guess she doesn't want me to mess up anymore."

She got it. She smiled and we prayed. I assume that taking a moment to consider the one who wrote her the letter has made all the difference in the world to her.

Have you ever wondered about the big God behind the Book as you read? Picture Him as you read and you won't need silly poltergeists to get the message across. Imagine God speaking to you in the pages Scripture and you will encounter Him.

 Choose a story from the four gospels and apply the four stages of Bible study to it (given at the end of the first week). You might want to take more time on this throughout the week and space it out or just try it in a block of time you have.

Look at the parable in Luke 16 carefully and share with your partner or group why you think Jesus told this story. What shortcoming, need or problem would necessitate a parable such as this?

Reflect on your experience with the trustworthiness of the Bible. When have you had to simply believe the words even though you didn't really feel that they were true or helpful?

Therefore everyone who hears these words of mine and puts them into practice is like a wise man who built his house on the rock. The rain came down, the streams rose, and the winds blew and beat against that house; yet it did not fall, because it had its foundation on the rock. But everyone who hears these words of mine and does not put them into practice is like a foolish man who built his house on sand. The rain came down, the streams rose, and the winds blew and beat against that house, and it fell with a great crash. (Matthew 7:24-27)

How do you know when you know something? I get a headache trying to chase the concept around in my mind. All I can come up with is the distinction between a shallow knowing versus a deep, experiential knowing.

I saw the difference between "knowing" and "really knowing" exposed in a college class on the life and teachings of Christ. Sometimes when we think we know something we still have much to learn. This principle rang true for a certain "Mr. Know-It-All".

In a class discussion on forgiveness, Mr. Know-It-All made a bold statement: "I think Scripture is clear. God won't forgive us until we forgive our enemies." And to a certain degree, he was right on. But the young lady sitting next to him blew up.

"My best friend was raped at a party. Have you ever had to forgive someone for doing something like that?"

The class went silent. The air ceased to move and Mr. Know-It-All missed the cue to remain quiet. Ignoring all the signals the class sent him, he opened his mouth to speak but before the second syllable left his lips the teacher cut him off abruptly;

"Let's think about this for a minute."

Mr. Know-It-All's life was saved by the teacher.

The class squirmed with awkward anticipation until the teacher said, "Pair up with the person sitting next to you and talk about why it seems too difficult to forgive our enemies and maybe share an experience where forgiving someone was especially difficult."

The class had been through moments like this before and were relatively comfortable with the assignment. Mr. Know-It-All turned away from the girl he so thoughtlessly offended but all the other students were paired up. He turned back slowly to face the stewing eyes of his "neighbor" boring into him.

She went first. She described the night her roommate returned from the party in tears. The police interview. The heartless denial of the perpetrator. The injustice. The smirks of everyone who knew. The whispers. Each phrase was like a blow to Mr. Know-It-All. She ended with, "I'm sorry, it is not your fault but how can you expect me forgive this guy?" For the first time in class Mr. Know-It-All had no "come back." The teacher watched him carefully in case he was under the misguided impression that he was a cat with eight more lives to spare. But Mr. Know-It-All learned a lesson that morning that he would never forget. There are those who know and those who simply think they know.

My Dad is a carpenter. As a boy I would work "with" him. Most of the time, I watched and stayed out of the way. Pounding a four-inch nail into a board in three swift, well placed hits looked pretty easy. Cutting a straight line with an electric saw seemed as easy as holding the wood and hitting the switch. When he would say, "You want to give it a try?" I'd leap into action. He tried to coach me but I wasn't listening. I was building. The nail would bend, the saw would bind, my grip would tire and the whole building experience would become less glamorous. It looked so easy.

Applying the truths of Scripture can be equally difficult. As we crack open the Bible and search for a significant message we are struck with the notion that "this isn't all that easy." Knowing what to do and doing it are two different things. Believe me, it is much easier to hand over the hammer and give back the saw. Likewise, we might be tempted close the Bible too soon because it is simply not that engaging. Murray Hunter once said that the Bible was not meant to be read as much as consumed. Novels pull you in and trap you with fantasy and plots but the Holy Scriptures invite you to search and struggle with what God is trying to say to people. It may even be true that the message of the Bible must be tried in order for it to teach.

Look at the parable of the two foundations: Both endure the fierce blistering of bad weather. The rain, wind and water come with full force. What makes the difference? The foundation. One is built on the shaky soil of just hearing and not doing. The house built on the rock is based on the life that hears and does what Christ says.

It is not enough to believe, understand, know, agree, feel, acknowledge, or accept what the Bible says. All these activities can be done without lifting a finger. Actively doing what God's word says is not about righteousness by works over faith or vice versa. It is about overcoming the lifelessness that comes from a lack of experience.

Do you want the words of Scripture to change your life or simply inform it? You have to work. Forgiving the unforgivable is hard work, but God's grace will always seem cheap until you actually experience how much it costs to give it away. Speaking words of kindness when you want to pummel someone with profanities requires more than simply remembering a verse or two. It demands all of you. Honor your Father and Mother; sounds easy enough while they are watching—but what about when no one else can see? Allowing others to be first makes good sense when it doesn't cost you much—but it's easy to tuck the verse away if it might mean missing a promotion or making the team.

The Christian walk that makes your muscles sore is the result of faith at work. Beware of the sneaky seduction of thinking God just wants you to agree with something that is true or understand a truth that is complex. When it comes to knowing God's will through the Bible, hearing and doing are inseparable activities.

 Think about the parts of your Christian experience that you may know, but that aren't really part of your normal practice as a Christian. Make a list of a few things you want to do in response to what you know in the words of the Bible. Try it out today. Be a doer.

Reflect on the struggle of doing God's Word. What happened throughout the day and what experiences did you face?

[1] Dallas Willard, The Spirit of the Disciplines, (New York: Harper Collins Publishers 1988), p. 198.

[2] Richard Foster, Celebration of Discipline (New York: Harper Collins Publisher, 1988), p. 33.

[3] E.M. Bounds, The Complete Works of E.M. Bounds on Prayer, (Grand Rapids, Michigan: Baker, 1992), p. 447.

[4] Jon Dybdahl, Hunger: Satisfying the Longing of Your Soul (Hagerstown, MD: Autumn House Publishing [A division of Review and Herald], 2008), p. 68.

[5] Dallas Willard, The Spirit of the Disciplines, (New York: HarperCollins, 1988), p. 177.

[6] Jaqueline Salmon, Washington Post: June 24, 2008).

[7] Michael P. Green, 1500 Illustrations for Biblical Preaching (Grand Rapids, Michigan: Baker Book, 2000), p. 100.

[8] Ellen White, Great Controversy (Pacific Press Publishing Association, Mountain View, CA) , p. 525.

[9] William A. Dembski, Intelligent Design: The Bridge Between Science & Theology, (Downers Grove, Illinois: InterVarsity Press, 1999) p. 25.

[10] Stuart Hample & Eric Marshall, Children's Letters to God, (New York: Workman Publishing, 1991) p. 40.

[11] Michael P. Green, 1500 Illustrations for Biblical Preaching, (Grand Rapids, Michigan: Baker, 2000) p. 79.

Small Group Questions—PRAYER AND GUIDANCE THROUGH SCRIPTURE

Pray for each other, randomly until everyone has been thoughtfully prayed for or go around the circle and pray for the person on your left, to remain faithful to this challenge and to be changed by the whole experience. Or, If your group is well acquainted, go around and share what you want God to do in you on this journey and share also what you would like your friends to do to keep you active in this group.

When you pray, how would characterize the content of your prayers?
What do you pray for the most? What do you pray for the least?

When in your life has your prayer life been rich?
Why do you think this season was so meaningful?

Share an "ah-ha" moment in studying the Bible where you discovered something that you never heard or seen before. What was your response to your discovery and how has that discovery impacted your understanding of how God guides in Scripture?

Share a book of the Bible or a section of the Bible that you might have avoided because of certain challenges that were in the text. How does the difficulty of Bible study affect our willingness to study?

Who has inspired you with their personal approach to studying?
What is it about their approach that you admire? Who do you know that applies Scripture to their life consistently and with integrity? How does their devotion to study influence their daily life?

What was the most helpful insight you gained from your study this week?

What would you like your partner/partners to pray for as you enter a new week and a new discipline?

To close the study you may want to pray as a group and encourage everyone to pray for the person on their left.

BIBLE STUDY—A Phased Approach

As you consider various approaches to studying the Bible you will notice that most of the devotional approaches are quite similar. The following is a process that is helpful to me:

PHASE 1—Look at God's Word

· With eyes that are open, observe the details in the text. The words, phrases, names, verbs, emotions, contrasts, lists, conditions. Most of the work is detective business—looking for the pieces of the puzzle. You might try underlining, circling, or highlighting specific things you notice or drawing lines to connect ideas in a chapter.

· With eyes that wonder, picture the reality of the event or conversation with your mind's eye. Envision the encounter.

· With eyes that focus, ruminate on one idea, thought or section at a time.

PHASE 2—Listen to God's Word

· With ears to their world, try to understand what the writer meant to say in their time and place.

· With the ears of your world, sense the relevance of God's Word for you. This exercise is one of bridge building!

· With ears to recognize, catch the sound of God's voice speaking to your heart and life personally.

PHASE 3—Learn from God's Word

· With a balanced mind, measure each passage in light of the whole of Scripture.

· With a practical mind, determine the areas of your life that need renewal and how that might occur.

· With a proactive mind, seek to live differently in light of discovery.

PHASE 4—Live God's Word

· With personal application, directly relate your scenario and sphere of influence to scripture.

· With a pliable heart, be willing to be shaped by your study throughout the day.

· With a provable response, act out God's Word. (This is a specific response that you can identify. I can say, "I want to control my temper!" but a provable application would be, "I'm going to control my temper in the game tonight and practice self mastery.")

—WEEK 2—
Service and Being Alone/Quiet

Service

If you are a "doer," then the discipline of service may not feel as much like a discipline as other exercises will. I've often wondered why serving others seems to strike a sweet chord in the hearts of humans. I wonder if service resonates because we were created in God's image and we possess the capacity to be selfless—like God. Maybe, as we help others we finally feel like we fit into the skin God created for us. If so, selfishness is an awkward fit but over time we may just learn to live it until we feel normal wearing a skin we were not meant for.

It's time to get out of the house and "do" something, but don't run too far ahead because you might want to consider the difference between service and becoming a servant. The two ideas are connected, but sometimes people serve others without becoming a servant.

Most people are at their best when they are serving others. Most people, I would guess, learn what it means to become a servant on the journey of serving others. Think about what the word "servant" actually implies:

A person bound in servitude to another human being as an instrument of labor; one who has lost his liberty and has no rights.[1]

The definition is simple to comprehend, the attitude of a servant is often hard to attain. Nevertheless, the beautiful work of helping others has a way of transforming not just our actions, but our minds about our relationship to humanity.

The truth is, people feel alive when they spend themselves for someone in need. Young and old are made full with joy when they can help someone else in a tangible way. For many, serving others is a joy and not a "discipline." Service can be a selfish exercise when the doer is only after the satisfaction of a job well done. To "do" acts of kindness just to build the muscle of service in the spiritual life can be misleading if obtaining the heart of a servant is not the goal.

However, choosing to serve when the motivation is not natural is truly an exercise that honors God and strengthens character.

As we practice this discipline, it is encouraging to be reminded that according to the Savior, there is no greater activity to undertake in the days in which we live than to feed the hungry, visit the lonely and comfort the hurting as stated in Matthew 25:34-36:

"Then the King will say to those on his right, 'Come, you who are blessed by my Father; take your inheritance, the kingdom prepared for you since the creation of the world. For I was hungry and you gave me something to eat, I was thirsty and you gave me something to drink, I was a stranger and you invited me in, I needed clothes and you clothed me, I was sick and you looked after me, I was in prison and you came to visit me.'"

Being Alone/Quiet

The discipline of solitude may prove to be the most difficult exercise for some; it just doesn't fit anywhere in our lifestyle. Being alone and being quiet are not even luxuries in our society—they are anomalies. Those who remove themselves from rapid flow of life's endeavors often find clarity of mind and a resolute joy that becomes precious to the soul.

Initially it is easy to think of solitude as loneliness. Richard Foster clarifies the difference between solitude and loneliness:

"Solitude is more a state of mind and heart than it is a place. There is a solitude of the heart that can be maintained at all times…It is quite possible to be a desert hermit and never experience solitude. But if we possess inward solitude we do not fear being alone, for we know that we are not alone. Neither do we fear being with others, for they do not control us. In the midst of the noise and confusion we are settled into a deep inner silence. Whether alone or among people, we always carry with us a portable sanctuary of the heart.

We have developed a phobia of being alone. We prefer the most trivial and even obnoxious company, the most meaningless activities, to being alone with ourselves; we seem to be frightened at the prospect of facing ourselves."[2]

The challenge of choosing moments of solitude comes not because we don't have time, but because we don't value the discipline as much as other activities. For many, moving into substantial periods of quietness is a constricting experience, but Dallas Willard discusses how liberating solitude can be.

"Solitude frees us, actually. This above all explains its primacy and priority among the disciplines. The normal course of day-to-day human interactions locks us into pattern of feeling, thought and action that are geared to a world set against God…In Solitude we find the psychic distance, the perspective from which we can see, in the light of eternity, the created things that trap, worry, and oppress us.[3]

Hopefully, as we face the challenge of solitude this week, we will be diligent to cut away some quality time. But be reminded, this is a journey and not a test. We need the time alone, but we don't need to flog ourselves if we experience failure or disappointment in the process. Set some goals and encourage your partner(s) to be aware of the challenges with being quiet and alone. Commit to stay through the awkward moments of solitude and stretch your comfort zone.

DAY 8 · VISIBLE FAITH

A few days later, when Jesus again entered Capernaum, the people heard that he had come home. So many gathered that there was no room left, not even outside the door, and he preached the word to them. Some men came, bringing to him a paralytic, carried by four of them. Since they could not get him to Jesus because of the crowd, they made an opening in the roof above Jesus and, after digging through it, lowered the mat the paralyzed man was lying on. When Jesus saw their faith, he said to the paralytic, "Son, your sins are forgiven." (Mark 2:1-5)

The sun beat down on everyone at the park that blistering summer day. Three brothers came to drink deep from the water fountain. I waited in line for my turn at the well as the two older brothers stood tightly on their tiptoes stretching their tongues toward the stream of cool water. The youngest cried out, "Water. Me want drink, too." Being next in line and very thirsty, I was already prepared to lift the toddler for a drink. So, more out of impatience and less out of kindness, I made my move to lift the toddler toward the water. But I was too late; the older brothers were on it even as I opened my mouth to volunteer.

The boys each took an arm of the toddler and tried to prop the little one upward enough to reach the faucet. Their efforts were valiant but their arms could only sustain their little brother for a moment, but not long enough to drink. It was time I intervened.

"Let me give him a hand." I said.

They wouldn't have it. I'll never forget what I saw next. My heart was touched as the oldest brother got down on his hands and knees like a dog next to the wet, rocky fountain, while the other lad lifted the thirsty child onto his brother's back like he was a step stool. The older brother supported the slurping toddler with one hand and pushed the button for water with the other. The other brother on his hands and knees laughed as the water trickled down the side of the fountain, totally soaking the side of big brother below. After an enormous amount of water filled the thirsty child, he jumped down—the brothers got up laughing and they ran off together, soaking wet, but full.

The three brothers at the park remind me of the story of the healing of the paralytic recorded in Mark 2:1-5. You don't have look too deep into the story to discover its central message. Four friends get together to help another friend who was paralyzed. The four made sure their friend made it to the feet of Jesus. Their reward? The work! Their joy? The look on their friend's face when Jesus said,

"You are forgiven." The unforgettable lesson? Do whatever it takes to bring thirsty people to the One who has water.

Selfless service is simply a way of life for believers. Serving people is the basic marching order that came from Christ. Few things give us a sense of rightness, a feeling of being full of Christ-like kindness. Doing whatever it takes to help someone. Can you imagine how the four felt? Notice what it says about them;

"When Jesus saw their faith, he said to the paralytic, "Son, your sins are forgiven." Let us not limit our help to the tangible things that can be bought, baked or given, but include the intangible service Christ freely gave the paralytic—forgiveness. It is no little thing to offer forgiveness for sins, which is why Jesus met the objections of the religious leaders with: "Which is easier to say to this paralyzed man, 'Your sins are forgiven,' or to say, 'Get up, take your mat and walk'?" (Mark 2:9) What Jesus does in forgiving the man and in healing his paralysis is a moot point if four friends don't bring him to Christ.

Some wonder if the little things they do for others really matter. According to Jesus, our kindness counts. God does the counting; we do the kindness.

The story is told of a piccolo player playing in a symphony. It occurred to her that the sound of her piccolo was so small and insignificant that she couldn't possibly be needed? She decided to stop playing and, as she put her instrument away, the conductor stopped the practice, "What happened to the piccolo? I don't hear the second piccolo!" he thundered. The piccolo player was shocked that amid the noise of the symphony, the conductor could hear each instrument. The same is true with our service to others. Big or small, God hears.

The discipline of service is simple: Look for a need, then meet it. Find a way to help someone who is struggling. Be creative, but be thorough. Take some risks. Tear up a roof. Do whatever it takes.

Make it a point to be on the lookout for service opportunities. Today, in the middle of the mundane everyday routine, seek out an opportunity to do the smallest thing for someone else. Don't make the mistake of thinking that your contribution will never change the world. The world changes for the better by one selfless act of service at a time.

Think about the times you have felt closest to God. What were you doing? Were you just sitting there in church? Or on a mountain? Why do you think Jesus spent so much time with the people who needed help?

DAY 9 · CUPS OF COOL WATER

Teacher," said John, "we saw a man driving out demons in your name and we told him to stop, because he was not one of us." "Do not stop him," Jesus said. "No one who does a miracle in my name can in the next moment say anything bad about me, for whoever is not against us is for us. I tell you the truth, anyone who gives you a cup of water in my name because you belong to Christ will certainly not lose his reward. (Mark 9:38-41)

It was a little irritating to the disciples, I presume. Some upstart doing the things Jesus said they were supposed to do. The disciples were chosen and trained. The upstart wasn't picked. He never came to class. Clearly, he never experienced the miraculous moments that led all twelve of the disciples to the side of Jesus. Were the imposter's acts of goodness really good? Who was this "other man" who drove away demons in Jesus name? The identity of the "extra-other-guy" is not revealed in Scripture. So, what was the problem?

The problem was in the attitude of the disciples. They just got a lesson on humility and being a servant. What were they thinking? The disciples were probably thinking along a similar path that many of us wander down: The path of selective service. We are willing to serve, but when being a servant takes us somewhere we don't feel comfortable going, the service is less enchanting. Kenneth Fleming tells the story of his personal discovery of what it means to be a servant:

"Office boy—that was to be my position? A strong sensation of hurt welled up in me. I had been a missionary among the Zulu people in South Africa for just over two years. Zulu language and culture had largely occupied my time, along with pulling teeth, laying bricks, and teaching Scripture lessons in the local school. I had begun preaching simple messages in Zulu and generally being a helper to our senior missionary, Mr. Edwin Gibbs. He and his wife had just left for a furlough in the United States. Thus my wife and I were the only married missionaries on the station; I felt kind of a pleasure at being left "in charge." At last I was a real missionary.

Now at the quarterly conference, some of the Zulu leaders agreed that one of their number should assume the "position and authority" of Mr. Gibbs. Then a question arose as to the position of the new missionary—me. His position, they said, was to be "office boy."

...My defenses popped up. Most of them couldn't even read. Didn't they know the lifestyle we had left behind in America to be here? What connection could there possibly be between being an "office boy" and the work of ministry I was called to do?

Just then my best Zulu friend, Isaac Zindela, took me aside…"

"Don't be upset by what you heard tonight. Just remember what Jesus said to the disciples in Mark chapter ten, verse forty five." It was a verse I knew by heart in English. But now he quoted it deliberately and slowly in Zulu, every word made me feel like a man being pelted with stones in Bible times. For even the Son of man did not come to be served, but to serve, and to give His life as a ransom for many.[4]

Jesus delivers a condition for discipleship in one simple sentence when he stated, "If anyone wants to be first, he must be the very last, and the servant of all" (Mark 9:35)

I'm not sure what the word "all" means in the Greek but I'm guessing it probably means: All. Everyone. Not just those who are easy to serve or those for whom we feel like we are making a difference.

If anyone has been a servant to all, it is John Perkins. While enduring a season of racial tyranny, his life is a testimony of service to all. Imagine how hard it was for John to swallow his hatred in light of his childhood experience where his brother Clyde, was senselessly killed by an officer of the law:

The fuse had been lit and the explosion was about to occur on that Saturday, for Clyde had returned from the War determined to stand up for himself. He raised his voice while waiting in line for the theatre to open and inspired a typically controlling response from the deputy marshall: "You niggers quiet down." Instead of silently acquiescing, Clyde [John's older brother] tried to speak to the law officer. The deputy reacted to this hint of insubordination by clubbing Clyde. Moving to defend himself from further attack, Clyde grabbed the baton. The deputy, now completely overtaken by his rage, stepped back and shot him twice in the stomach. The shots were fatal…Big brother Clyde had been John's model, his mentor, his hero, and his companion. All the children of his generation looked up to Clyde. He had donned his country's uniform, had been wounded several times in the bloody war against the Germans, and had returned with ribbons and a Purple Heart, to celebrate the allied victory among his people. Having proved his manly valor on the battlefield, he came back to a racist system that denied him his very personhood. Having helped cleanse the world of Hitler's racism, he had returned to a place where he received treatment similar to what a Jew would experience under the Nazi regime. This was the supreme irony for the black soldier in World War II."[5]

John Perkins, although embittered with hatred, became a servant of God and ultimately a giant in the service of his community. Perkins has devoted his life to transforming local communities with dignity and pride. In spite of obstacles of prejudice and short-sighted thinking, John Perkins is a leader for community transformation. His story sears through the petty problems I have with annoying people and rearranges the hierarchies inherent to my worldview. My prayer is to have the heart of Christ who became a servant to all and instructed anyone who followed Him to do likewise.

Who do you enjoy serving? Who, in your world, is difficult to serve? God wants us all to "go there." "All" still means "all" and "go" still means "go" when it comes to a life of service in the wilderness.

 Serve someone who is difficult to serve. You can do it openly or in secret. Give a helping hand when your guts scream out, 'I don't want to" or "I don't like that person."

Identify in your own heart of hearts the people who you really struggle to be servant-minded toward. Reflect on the qualities that make them precious to God. Reflect on the thoughts you have toward the people who irritate you and talk to God in your reflections about changing your heart.

DAY 10 · ENORMOUS LITTLE THINGS

When the Son of Man comes in his glory, and all the angels with him, he will sit on his throne in heavenly glory. All the nations will be gathered before him, and he will separate the people one from another as a shepherd separates the sheep from the goats. He will put the sheep on his right and the goats on his left. Then the King will say to those on his right, "Come, you who are blessed by my Father; take your inheritance, the kingdom prepared for you since the creation of the world. For I was hungry and you gave me something to eat, I was thirsty and you gave me something to drink, I was a stranger and you invited me in, I needed clothes and you clothed me, I was sick and you looked after me, I was in prison and you came to visit me." Then the righteous will answer him, "Lord, when did we see you hungry and feed you, or thirsty and give you something to drink? When did we see you a stranger and invite you in, or needing clothes and clothe you? When did we see you sick or in prison and go to visit you?" The King will reply, "I tell you the truth, whatever you did for one of the least of these brothers of mine, you did for me." (Matt 25:31-46)

What a surprise! It is amazing to think how the little things we do are really the most important endeavors in the grand scheme of things.

In *The Seven Habits of Highly Effective People*, Stephen Covey reflects on how he learned the surprising value of "little things" on a rather ordinary evening with his two sons. They did a variety of things, ending with a movie. Four-year-old Sean fell asleep during the movie, and when it was over, Covey picked him up in his arms, carried him to the car, and laid him in the back seat. It was very cold that evening, so he took off his coat and gently arranged it around the boy. Later that evening it came time to tuck in six-year-old Stephen. Covey tried to talk to him about the evening, to find out what he had liked the most, but there was little response. Suddenly little Stephen turned over on his side, facing the wall, and started to cry.

"What's wrong, honey? What is it?" asked Covey.

The boy turned back, chin quivering, eyes wet. "Daddy," he asked, "if I were cold, would you put your coat around me, too?"

Covey wrote, "Of all the events of that special night out together, the most important was a little act of kindness—a momentary, unconscious showing of love to his little brother."[6]

In the grand finale of His description of "the end," Jesus points to little acts of kindness as the last word on the subject. The parable of the sheep and the goats tells the tale of those who make it in the end. What is striking about the story is the fact that they don't know they've arrived—they are surprised by the final score. They ask the Lord "When, when did I feed you, clothe you, visit you?" Fishing for compliments? I don't think so.

These chosen sheep are picked because of their *compassion.* Compassion is a medical word describing the workings of the intestinal region. Of all the metaphors and illustrations that were available in the human anatomy, God chose the innards. Guts. The word implies having your insides twist and cry out. Seeing someone in need causes an internal pain from your innermost part, and the only appropriate thing to do is help. Completely unaware that someone might be watching, they focus on fixing the pain. They move to act on behalf of others because they are moved deep within by compassion.

When Jesus says, "When I was naked you clothed me..." it is a surprise to them. Doing acts of service and becoming a servant can be two different pathways. One path begins with a list and a scorecard, the other starts with a desire to be like Jesus and feed, serve, visit, give, comfort and build people, without a ledger.

There are a couple of insights that grow out of this parable: 1) Do the *little things* because that is our part, and 2) Do the little things *for Christ* who has already done the biggest part.

LITTLE THINGS

Christ calls us to meet the basic needs of broken people. Hungry? Feed them. Lonely? Stay with them. Sick? Help them become whole again. Do what may seem to be *a little thing.* Often, we long for our service to be comprehensive, exhaustive, and unmistakably significant. Maybe we want the cost of our service to count. We expect some tangible result from the time and energy we expend for someone else. If you were to offer food or drink, clothing or comfort to someone who is in need you may feel like you didn't really "make a difference" in an enduring way. When we do the little things with the mindset that we are cooperating with a God who is doing the big things, our service makes good sense.

THE REASON—CHRIST

Jesus claims that as we serve people, we serve Him. In a sense, we cooperate with His great work in a way we can offer help. Throughout the ministry of Jesus He healed, helped, fed, found, and fixed the broken parts of people, not in hopes of "changing the world" one act of kindness at a time, but in order to change our minds about God. The overwhelming message to the hungry, blind, leprous, and lost was: God cares and He has power to make what is broken new again. God's work in saving humanity from their sin is depicted and replayed in a small way every time we do the little things. What we do for others we do out of our love and adoration of Christ who has made a way for all to come to eternal life.

So, if you are going to count anything as you serve, count each person as though they were Christ incognito. Do the little things you can do in full view of the great things God has done for all.

> Practice in a very specific way one of the service activities of the "sheep" in Matthew 25 and share with your partner what you did. Or, plan to do this with a friend and serve another person as the sheep in the parable. Interview someone who serves in one of the "sheep" activities and ask them what is meaningful about their work? When have you kept score or done an act of kindness for ulterior motives? Why is it difficult to see people around you as though they are "Christ in Person?"

DAY 11 · MIRRORING THE MIND OF CHRIST

 Then Jesus went up on a mountainside and sat down with his disciples. The Jewish Passover Festival was near. When Jesus looked up and saw a great crowd coming toward him, he said to Philip, "Where shall we buy bread for these people to eat?" He asked this only to test him, for he already had in mind what he was going to do. (John 6:4-6)

 As a young child I played competitive soccer in youth leagues and I learned early on that coaches can ask you to do crazy things, and there is not much you can do to stop them. While we were resting on the grass at halftime our coach commanded us to "get up and hop around while waving our arms up and down." We looked ridiculous, but later I learned the coach was trying to keep our muscles from seizing up with lactic acid because we had another game soon after. Another coach made us chew on the orange peels we had as snacks at halftime. Why? I later found out that the oil in the peels coats the inside your mouth keeping you from feeling like your mouth is stuffed with cotton. Cools tricks.

HAVING THE MIND OF CHRIST

Wouldn't you like to know what Christ was thinking?

Paul says it well in what was thought to be a Christian hymn:

"Therefore if you have any encouragement from being united with Christ, if any comfort from his love, if any common sharing in the Spirit, if any tenderness and compassion, then make my joy complete by being like-minded, having the same love, being one in spirit and of one mind. Do nothing out of selfish ambition or vain conceit. Rather, in humility value others above yourselves, not looking to your own interests but each of you to the interests of the others.

In your relationships with one another, have the same mindset as Christ Jesus:

Who, being in very nature God,

did not consider equality with God

something to be used to his own advantage;

rather, he made himself nothing

by taking the very nature of a servant,

being made in human likeness.

And being found in appearance as a man,

he humbled himself

by becoming obedient to death—

even death on a cross! (Philippians 2:1-8)

What would it be like to have a "mind like Christ?" Keith Green penned these words in a song to convey his passion to submit to Christ with a servant's heart.

The end of all my prayers is to care like my Lord cares

My one and only cause his image in my soul

well I'm blind to others needs

and I'm tired of planting seeds

I seem to have a wealth of so many thoughts about myself.

I want to

I need to

Be more like Jesus

I learned a little bit about having a servant's heart by watching some children at school:

Lunchtime. Outside of recess and P.E., there are few competing highlights of the school day. I was visiting my wife while she worked on developing a remedial program for students. I found myself spending lunchtime in the first grade. I enjoyed watching the students rustle around the classroom with their lunch pails and small boxes of milk. I noticed one boy with bright red curly hair who remained in his seat while everyone else busied themselves with food. My heart sank into my stomach as someone announced out loud what was obvious to anyone watching, "Billy doesn't have a lunch."

At first I thought the remark was cruel. Before I could react, the room full of students scurried into action. What I saw seared the most beautiful image of community into my mind. Each student began breaking off pieces of their peanut butter and jelly sandwiches and placed them on a tray that was being passed around the room. I never saw who started the tray. Bags of chips popped open and littered the brown plastic cafeteria tray with samples of every flavor known to first graders across the land. The tray was loaded with a half of a banana, also what seemed to be tons of carrots and celery, and a bounty of cookies broken in half. As the tray filled with food was set before the hungry lad, a grin crept shyly across his sweet, freckled face. Embarrassed? A little. Tickled to death at the feast fit for five first graders looming before him like a small mountain? No question about it.

Actually, I had many questions. Who started the tray? When did they learn to do this? Why didn't I forget my lunch? I asked the teacher, "Where did they learn to do this?" He smiled, "It happened a few years back when one of my students shared his lunch with anyone who forgot theirs. Everyone joined in and then it just became kind of an unspoken rule in the classroom. When someone forgets a lunch, everyone helps." I was stunned by the simple way the kids created community in their classroom.[7]

The problem with wanting a servant's heart is that some people hope for an instantaneous transplant when the work of heart transformation is gradual. They pray, "Lord, just help me to be nice to that mean person." The answer to that prayer may be an awkward encounter where they have the opportunity to practice being nice when they feel like being mean. The road to change is not paved by tickling sensations down your spine as much as it is hard work. Again, remember the words of the Master Teacher, "…anyone who is rightly trained will become like the teacher." (Luke 6:40)

Some have a gift for feeling the needs of others, but having the gift doesn't necessarily mean they have a "servant's heart." The discipline of following through on the little things shapes the contours of the heart, fashioning it into the likeness of Christ. The more they are open to the shaping process, the less they feel inconvenienced by the needs of others.

 Try serving someone in a way that takes a little planning. Instead of a serendipitous event, premeditate an act of grace for someone in the name of Christ.

Share your thoughts and feelings on the topic of personal growth and how hard it is to have a servant's heart. What do you struggle with most? What moments in your journey affirm a servant's heart in your life?

DAY 12 · WHEN AND WHERE

 Very early in the morning, while it was still dark, Jesus got up, left the house and went off to a solitary place, where he prayed. Simon and his companions went to look for him, and when they found him, they exclaimed: "Everyone is looking for you!" Jesus replied, "Let us go somewhere else—to the nearby villages—so I can preach there also. That is why I have come." So he traveled throughout Galilee, preaching in their synagogues and driving out demons. (Mark 1:29-39)

 A young boy in India once observed a man praying on the riverbank: "When the holy man completed his prayer the boy went over and asked him, "Will you teach me to pray?" The holy man studied the boy's face carefully. Then he gripped the boys head in his hands and plunged it forcefully into the water! The boy struggled frantically, trying to free himself in order to breathe, he gasped, "What did you do that for?" The holy man said: "I just gave you your first lesson." "What do you mean?" asked the astonished boy. "Well," said the holy man, "when you long to pray as much as you longed to breathe when your head was underwater—only then will I be able to teach you to pray."[8]

The holy man recognized that there is a type of praying that comes not from duty, but from desperation. When Jesus rose up early to pray something drove Him from sleep to His knees.

A craving to be alone. I crave many things, but silence and solitude? No way. I tend to crave solitude in the same way I hunger for overcooked asparagus. "Jesus went to a solitary place to pray." He "went" is probably a gross understatement. I think He was driven. If you look in the gospel of Mark at the day Jesus had before this moment, you can see why He would be desperate for solitude as though it were the only place he could breathe. All day He worked and continued into the night and, "while it was still dark," something moved Jesus to trade sleep to breathe more fully in the presence of God. What would you lose sleep for? A late night movie? A video game? Work? Studies?

The kind of communion that comes from solitude does not happen in a moment of quick reflection just before you race out the door. It happens when you walk away—completely; when you walk away from work, school, activities, ambitions, demands and disruptions so you can breathe. But walking away is not as much about leaving other things as it is about moving towards something else. Solitude. Silence. Being alone. Being still. Today, these qualities are not always considered values in society. Labels such as "recluse" or a "hermit" are not necessarily flattering terms used to describe a person who retreats. But God rewards those who seek Him.

It just seems wrong to call time spent in solitude a "retreat." "Retreat" is loaded with the language of defense instead of offense. It smacks of turning tail and running. The purpose of calling for a "retreat" in battle is to announce that you need to run for cover so you can regroup or try to survive the oncoming forces. The word "retreat" is a reaction when you think you are losing. I don't see this as the way Jesus drives himself to solitude. If there is a word that portrays Jesus' struggle to be alone, it's "Charge!" That's right. Yell, "Charge!" instead of "retreat!" because that is exactly what Jesus does when the challenges of life become overwhelming.

On at least six occasions in the gospels Jesus slips away for a "charge." Every time He returns from His solitude, Christ emerges clear about His purpose. Have you had any recent "time outs" where you came from the quiet with a clear sense about life?

Do you need to take a walk? A chance to find out who you are again and what you should be doing? Go to a quiet garden or a mountain trail. Find a spot away from the interruptions where you can find solitude, and stay there. Stay until you are honest with God about who you are and who He is. Stay until your self-sufficiency is stripped away by the honest work of introspection. Stay to repent—fully. Remain alone through the impatience you feel until you have peace. Abide in the quietness long enough to taste how different the air is, then stay longer so that when you walk back you are like a fish out of water. Stay until you long to pray intimately with God as though your life depended on it.

The first exercise in solitude is to be still, the second is to listen. Clear away some time. It doesn't have to start out as a long period, but an hour would be a good start. Make sure you plan time to be alone. Find a quiet place where you can be alone and begin to listen to God speaking to your heart. It may take a while, but let Him speak to you. The task of solitude is not to pray for a long time but to "Be still and know that He is God." (Psalm 46:10)

Reflect on your experience alone with God and what happens to you when you just listen. Describe your experience—the struggles and the joys.

DAY 13 · MOUNTAIN TOP MOMENTS

> Immediately Jesus made his disciples get into the boat and go on ahead of him to Bethsaida, while he dismissed the crowd. After leaving them, he went up on a mountainside to pray. When evening came, the boat was in the middle of the lake, and he was alone on land. (Mark 6:45-47)

When my friends and I would leave together for a Saturday night adventure, Matt's father would say, "Matt, remember who you are." While it was embarrassing for Matt, I recall that his father's reminder usually made him think twice about how he spent his evening. While we were not tuned into the dynamics of mob frenzy, Matt's father was savvy to the potential opportunities that presented themselves to clusters of boys on a Saturday night.

Mob frenzy. Reporters have referred to the horrific experience of out-of-control crowds. Almost like a drug that robs you of your will, mob frenzy allows mindless acts of violence and debauchery to occur with no real rationale.

In England, a mob of mothers made their children carry signs saying "kill the child-molestor" and "Do unto them..." I know the offense is vile, but the sight of a five-year-old picketing in the streets, chanting to execute a criminal seems criminal.

At concerts, political protests, ball games and other seemingly innocent public gatherings, psychologists and sociologists have been studying the phenomenon of mob frenzy and are baffled by the outcome—mindless, needless, unexpected, irrational behavior. The tendencies of a frenzied mob make the parties involved look like rats on speed.

Dallas Willard cites the illustration of rats in the research lab and the effects of amphetamines on their group and individual behavior:

"It takes twenty times more the amount of amphetamine to kill individual mice than it takes to kill them in groups...In groups they go off like popcorn or firecrackers. Western men and women, especially, talk a great deal about being individuals. But our conformity to social pattern is hardly less remarkable than that of mice—and just as deadly."[9]

Sometimes I think we live like rats on speed. The pace and expectations of our culture seem to have an unchecked, overarching influence on our lives. What may be missing is the individual. The self. People who are okay with being alone find freedom from being defined by their circumstances. In solitude they develop a resolution that is shaped and molded by their Maker. Look at Jesus dismissing the crowd and moving into the quietness of the mountains to being alone—again. Jesus isn't shy, nor is He sick of ministry. He enters into moments of solitude to be mindful of who He is.

Do you remember the words of the tempter in the wilderness? "If you are the Son of God." When the well-fed multitudes wanted to crown Him King, Jesus refused and sent them away. Do you remember the jeers of the religious elite while Jesus hung on the cross? "If you are the Son of God—save yourself!" Jesus was clear about "who" He was and therefore knew that His purpose wasn't to save Himself from the cross but "give His life as a ransom for many." Do you see how important your identity is to your mission in life? Who you are shapes what you do. Solitude has a way of reminding you of who you are.

Some great discoveries have been made because individuals were alone and quiet. Dr. Frederick Banting, exhausted by working several jobs to supplement his income, fell asleep as he was working on some thoughts on the disease of diabetes. Waking at about 2:00 a.m., he stole away to a quiet spot for a few moments and wrote down three sentences in his solitude. He eventually went back to sleep, but those three sentences led to the discovery of insulin.

Sometimes our identity and purpose get lost and only a journey into the quiet will uncover our true self. Sometimes the struggle for solitude is a single-minded determination to be about one thing.

That is why disciples of Christ today steal away from the noise of life into the quietness of solitude to become truly aware of who they are. Check it out. Christians who act decisively and courageously are usually people who know how to be quiet and alone.

Take time today to be alone and reflect on who you are as an individual. Even in the stillness, talk to God openly about who you are, your strengths and weaknesses, your hopes and dreams, your successes and failures. Consider the big decisions you have made in the last few years. Remember the words of Ray Pritchard, "We make decisions, and our decisions make us."

Reflect on your experience of communion with God in solitude. Describe the impact the moments in solitude had on your identity in Christ. What did you discover? What was unexpected?

DAY 14 · PRAYING THAT STAYS

One of those days Jesus went out to a mountainside to pray, and spent the night praying to God. (Luke 6:12)

Following a worship service where I was a guest speaker, a young couple came up to me from the congregation and said, "You remind us of a friend we had in college. Do you know Jerry?" I knew Jerry. He had been a mentor to me since I was eighteen years old. He was assigned to my home church as an intern youth pastor for six months. Six months is all he had and he spent a large chunk of that time with me. He deliberately prodded, pushed, and poked me in my spiritual walk and ultimately had the greatest impact on my decision to become a pastor. As a result of those six months, Jerry's character, and even some of his characteristics, have been tattooed on me.

I answered the couple, "Jerry and I are very good friends."

They responded, "I can tell, you talk and act just like him. You must have spent a lot of time with him."

Nothing against Jerry, but I'm not comfortable with the notion that I'm an imitator. However the truth is—we all are! We cannot help but be changed by those who shape us. We cannot avoid the marking of our characters by people whose lives we admire. We cannot distance ourselves as students from the teachers we choose in life. Jesus said, "The student is not above the teacher, but everyone who is rightly trained will become like the teacher". (Luke 6:40) Like it or not, I'm like Jerry. Why? I spent time with him. I learned from him. I grew because of my friendship with him. In the same way mentors shape us, God marks us and transforms us in seasons of communion He has with us.

We often think of the spiritual exercise of solitude as a way of "spending time with God." Klaus Issler writes from a similar point of view:

To deepen our relationship with God, we must become comfortable in new ways of connecting with God, in "wasting time" with God. Although wasting time is generally considered a Western sin, for the Christian, wasting time with God is always good and right.[10]

Whether it is "spending time" or "wasting time," taking enough time is crucial to generating meaningful solitude. Since solitude involves listening to God as well as talking to Him, you need to be patient. Listening can be very inconvenient. You know what is like to enter into a conversation with a "gusher," knowing that the source of the emotional geyser may take a while to surface. Effective communion with God depends on people becoming desperate to listen.

Not hoping. Not desiring. Not expecting. Desperate.

Unfortunately, our culture is not a listening culture but a debating culture. Consider the conversations you have in an average day. In the exchange, to what degree do you listen to someone seeking only to understand them? Most of the time, we have another discussion happening within us about what we think, feel or believe—while the other person is still talking.

A significant number of popular "legitimate" news-related programs as well as afternoon talk shows set up gladiatorial–like formats. People with opposing views are pitted against each other and encouraged to fight it out. The less they listen to one another, the more they interrupt, the louder they shout, and the more polarized their views become, presumably, the more "successful" the program is.[11]

Is it possible that our cultural tendency to debate affects our communication with God? If we can't listen and learn well from each other, how do we expect to communicate with God?

Consider the following questions:

• Do you finish your prayer when you run out of things to say?

• How much of your praying is repeating phrases, topics and requests?

• Compare the prayers that have been powerful in your spiritual journey with the prayers that have left you feeling uncertain or ambiguous about the exchange. What made the difference?

It is also part of solitude to simply sense God's presence and His matchless love toward you. When you live in the presence of God, that presence has a way of sticking to you. Maybe that is why people were so drawn to Jesus. Maybe it was because He looked and sounded so much like the Father. Maybe just being near Jesus felt like being close to heaven. Jesus couldn't help but become tattooed by God's presence. Maybe He talked a bit. More likely, He listened to and remembered the words of Scripture. Maybe He spent those nights simply baking in the warm air of God's amazing love.

The change in your that so many long for comes not from one event or from some victorious experience, but from the deliberate commitment to being quiet and alone with God, for as long as it takes.

First, find a night when you can be alone with God for a long period of time. Allow God to speak to your heart through Scripture. Listen for His voice. Communicate with God as a Friend in conversation. Practice the presence of God for a significant period of time. (This will not just happen—plan it!)

What insights into your relationship with God grew out of this experience? Reflect on the power of solitude in your life as you have now experimented with it. How do you see the discipline of solitude becoming part of your spiritual life?

[1]   Nelson's Illustrated Bible Dictionary, Copyright (c)1986, Thomas Nelson Publishers.

[2]   Richard Foster, Celebration of Discipline, (New York: HarperCollins, 1988), p.96, 97.

[3]   Dallas Willard, The Spirit of the Disciplines, (New York: HarperCollins, 1988), p. 160, 161.

[4]   Kenneth C. Fleming, He Humbled Himself, (Westchester, Illinois: Crossway Books, 1989), p. 19,20.

[5]   Stephen E. Berk, A Time To Heal, (Grand Rapids, Michigan: Baker Books, 1997), p. 40.

[6]   Robert J. Morgan, Nelson's Complete Book of Stories, Illustrations, and Quotes, (Nashville, Tennessee: Thomas Nelson, 2000), p. 510.

[7]   Troy Fitzgerald, Christwise Discipleship Guide, (Hagerstown, Maryland: Review and Herald, 2002), p. 71.

[8]   James S. Hewitt, Illustrations Unlimited, (Tyndale House, 1990), p. 422.

[9]   Dallas Willard, The Spirit of the Disciplines, (New York: HarperCollins, 1988), p. 160, 161.

[10] Klaus Issler, Wasting Time With God, (Inter Varsity Press, Downers Grove, Ill, 2001), p. 30.

[11] Deborah L. Flick, From Debate to Dialogue, (Boulder, Colorado: Orchid Publications, 1998), p. 8.

Small Group Questions—SERVICE AND BEING ALONE/QUIET

When has someone given to you a gift of service and what difference did it make in your life?

What has been your greatest moment in service?
Describe how the experience shaped your life.

What kinds of service activities do you feel are most helpful in sharing the gospel?

When is service a discipline?
When is it something you don't really have to think much about?
Describe both scenarios.

Can you think of others who naturally serve and those who choose to integrate service as a way of life?

What are some service experiences you want to have in the coming week?

What kinds of gifts do you want to give to people in the way of service?

What do you look forward to when you approach scheduled times of solitude? What are some things that make you anxious?

In your experience, how much time do you think you need to be able to settle down and commune with God?

What do you find more difficult; being quiet and alone when you are alone or having a quiet heart throughout a normal day? Which do you find more meaningful? Why?

What are some of your expectations about times of solitude? What do you expect will happen in your heart and mind? What do you expect God to do in such times?

Talk with your partners about planning a "charge" where there will be ample time for renewal.

Worship and Fellowship

Worship

There is no mistaking the impact that worship can make in a believers life. Worship occurs when we choose to honor and ascribe worth to God. Worship is so personal that there are as many ways to worship God as there are worshippers. Perhaps Paul said it best when he wrote:

"Therefore, I urge you, brothers and sisters, in view of God's mercy, to offer your bodies as a living sacrifice, holy and pleasing to God—this is your true and proper worship." (Romans 12:1)

If our lives are not a living sacrifice then our weekly prayer, song, or offering is not really worship, it is entirely something else. William Temple, the Archbishop of Canterbury says this about worship:

Patrick Kavanaugh defines worship in the following manner:

"Worship is the submission of all our nature to God. It is the quickening of conscience by his holiness, nourishment of mind by his truth, purifying of the imagination by his beauty, opening of the heart to his love, and submission of will to his purpose. All this gathered up in adoration is the greatest of all expressions of which we are capable."[1]

Jesus, responding to the question, "What is the greatest commandment?" gave probably the most succinct definition of worship by quoting Deuteronomy 6:4-6:

"Hear, O Israel: The LORD our God, the LORD is one. Love the LORD your God with all your heart and with all your soul and with all your strength. These commandments that I give you today are to be upon your hearts."

It is hard to imagine a more complete description of worship than absolute devotion to God in all the areas of life. However, Dallas Willard describes in detail what this looks like in his definition of worship:

"In worship we engage ourselves with, dwell upon, and express the greatness, beauty, and goodness of God through thought and the use of words, rituals, and symbols. We do this alone as well as in union with God's people. To worship is to see God as worthy, to ascribe great worth to him."[2]

While worship is a holistic experience, our adoration of God is expressed through a variety of forms. Unfortunately, the forms can morph from being vehicles that carry our worship to God to empty religious routines or activities. When the forms fail to connect the worshipper to God, the tendency is to blame the form. The readings are dated. The hymns are too familiar. The prayers are impersonal. The relationship between the heart of worship and the forms of worship are crucial. Richard Foster notes:

"To say that forms are secondary is not to say that they are irrelevant. As long as we are finite human beings we must have forms. We must have "wineskins" that will embody our experience of worship. But the forms are not the worship; they only lead us into the worship."[3]

The tender balance between form and the heart is the only thing we have to keep our worship experience genuine. As we wrestle with the experience of worship it is to be expected that are lives will change by simply becoming intentional about the honor we ascribe to God. The ebb and flow of ideas about worship will always challenge the forms and the heart of worshippers, but hopefully in a way that edifies the church and honors God.

Fellowship

Fellowship is much more than a potluck dinner. The poet, John Donne, captures the essence of fellowship claiming, "No man is an island."

The terms "communion" and "fellowship" of the English Bible are varying translations of the words koinonia, and koinoneo, or their cognates. They designate acts of fellowship observed among the early Christians or express the unique sense of unity and fellowship of which these acts were the outward expression. The several passages in which these terms are used fall into two groups: those in which they refer to acts of fellowship, and those in which they refer to fellowship as experienced.[4]

I love how Solomon described the work of fellowship in Proverbs 27:17:

"As iron sharpens iron, so one man sharpens another."

A closer look at the Bible reveals that fellowship is much more than hanging out with buddies. Christian fellowship is designed to make us better people. Christian fellowship causes us to rise higher in our aspirations than we would alone. Paul demonstrates this dimension of fellowship in his heartfelt confession to his beloved church in Philippi:

"I thank my God every time I remember you. In all my prayers for all of you, I always pray with joy because of your partnership in the gospel from the first day until now, being confident of this, that he who began a good work in you will carry it on to completion until the day of Christ Jesus." (Philippians 1:3 6)

Spiritual partnership. Mutual investment. Integrity. Encouragement.

Accountability. Unity. Purpose. Collaboration. Growth. While there are dimensions of fellowship that are less intense compared to fasting or solitude, time honored teachers in spiritual formation claim:

"Our own natures tell us that people are not complete as isolated individuals. Humans move naturally to-ward each other. God created man for fellowship and because of that God gave him a wife, told them to multiply, and therefore formed the first unit of society. Community is part of God's purpose for humanity."[5]

"God intends the process of Spiritual formation to occur in a community context, so when we speak of spiritual formation through small groups, we really see spiritual formation in the normal context of Scripture—its natural setting is communal."[6]

Knowing what we know about how God created us, it is hard to imagine growth occurring in seclusion or isolation. Even more, some of the things God expects of His children can only happen as we work with one another.

"Fellowship" leaps from the pages of the Bible almost as frequently as the Second Coming of Christ or the Resurrection. Let the exercise of worship and fellowship saturate your life this week in a way that deepens the spiritual bonds you have with your brothers and sisters in Christ.

DAY 15 · THIS IS MY HOUSE!

Jesus entered the temple area and drove out all who were buying and selling there. He overturned the tables of the moneychangers and the benches of those selling doves. "It is written," he said to them, "'My house will be called a house of prayer,' but you are making it a 'den of robbers.'" The blind and the lame came to him at the temple, and he healed them. (Matthew 21:12-14)

What sets you off? What makes you angry? What kinds of behavior caused Jesus to go overboard? Throughout the gospels there are a handful of things that uncork deep emotion in the Son of God. Consider a few of times Jesus went overboard:

Jesus went **overboard** when people stand in the way of children coming to the Father.

"But if anyone causes one of these little ones who believe in me to sin, it would be better for him to have a large millstone hung around his neck and to be drowned in the depths of the sea." (Matthew 18:6)

Jesus went **overboard** over people who prejudge and spill out contempt for others.

"But I tell you that anyone who is angry with his brother will be subject to judgment. Again, anyone who says to his brother, 'Raca,' is answerable to the Sanhedrin. But anyone who says, 'You fool!' will be in danger of the fire of hell." (Matthew 5:22)

Jesus went **overboard** in the high standard he set for the way we forgive and give mercy to others.

"Then Peter came to Jesus and asked, "Lord, how many times shall I forgive my brother when he sins against me? Up to seven times?" Jesus answered, "I tell you, not seven times, but seventy-seven times." (Matthew 18:21-22)

Jesus went **overboard** in the unimaginable criteria for becoming a disciple.

"If anyone comes to me and does not hate his father and mother, his wife and children, his brothers and sisters—yes, even his own life—he cannot be my disciple." (Luke 14:26)

Jesus went **overboard** in the way that disciples should perceive the value and priority of His kingdom.

"Again, the kingdom of heaven is like a merchant looking for fine pearls. When he found one of great value, he went away and sold everything he had and bought it." (Matthew 13:45-46)

Jesus went **overboard** in His expectations of would-be followers.

"Jesus looked at him and loved him. "One thing you lack," he said. "Go, sell everything you have and give to the poor, and you will have treasure in heaven. Then come, follow me." (Mark 10:21)

Jesus went **overboard** with scandalous generosity for people who offend you.

Worship and Fellowship

"And if someone wants to sue you and take your tunic, let him have your cloak as well. If someone forces you to go one mile, go with him two miles." (Matthew 5:40-41)

Jesus went **overboard** in His hatred of the things that separate you and God.

"If your hand causes you to sin, cut it off. It is better for you to enter life maimed than with two hands to go into hell, where the fire never goes out." (Mark 9:43)

Perhaps the most famous moment of Jesus going **"overboard"** is in the temple when He encounters mindless bartering mixed with worship. Because the glory of God was shrouded in shortsighted stuff, Jesus sought to shake people from the trance of apathy to a sense of awe.

A similar effect was noted at the launch of Apollo 17. On a monumental night in 1975, hundreds of people gathered to witness the takeoff of this rocket that measured thirty-five stories in length. Many of the people that gathered to watch were skeptical and even verbally derisive about the whole project. Some were drinking and making jokes prior to the launch of the magnificent rocket. When the moment arrived and the countdown began, the revelry ceased and the crowd watched and waited.

Then, the bright orange light lit up the night sky so bright you could barely open your eyes. Only a moment after the light the roar of the engines engulfed the crowd as the rocket climbed slowly into the heavens. The scene can only be described as "awesome." The cynicism and frivolous talk vanished was replaced by awe and wonder. The witnesses of the launch were silent.

In Exodus 25:1 God said, "Have them make a sanctuary for me, and I will dwell among them," the intent was to stitch together the most awesome moment of all—God being present with people. Don't miss the irony when Jesus, "Immanuel"—"God with us" comes to the place where noise, business and banter buried the wonder of God's presence. I suppose God could have exploded on large gatherings of people and arrested everyone's attention by force. However, genuine worship grows out of a sense of God's worth—not fear or shame. When Jesus explodes on the temple fray with unmistakable zeal He is not out for revenge—He is after the hearts of people.

What tables need to be turned over in your life? I'm not talking about disruption for the sake of being a revolutionary. Jesus stormed the temple because somewhere hidden under the muck and melee of our noisy lives is a heart that might worship God out of adoration.

Think about the worship service that you attend. What kind of preparation do you want to have before you enter? How do you want to leave?

Think of a few things you can do to clear away the clutter and give God your full attention. Devise a specific ritual that enables you to clear the air of your heart and mind before you hand it over to God in worship.

Reflect on a worship experience where you felt that God had your full attention. What did it take and how did you feel? Think and write about what you can learn from the experiences you have had in worship up to this point in your journey.

DAY 16 · TRUE WORSHIPPER

 You Samaritans worship what you do not know; we worship what we do know, for salvation is from the Jews. Yet a time is coming and has now come when the true worshipers will worship the Father in spirit and truth, for they are the kind of worshipers the Father seeks. God is spirit, and his worshipers must worship in spirit and in truth." (John 4:20-26)

 Every time I read the story of Jesus and His conversation with the Samaritan woman I get stuck in the exchange they have about worship. Is Jesus saying that *all* Samaritans don't "get it" and the Jews do? Really? Then there is this cryptic statement about a coming day when "true worshippers" will come and "worship in spirit and truth." There must have been more to this conversation than what we have in John 4. Can you imagine this conversation between the Samaritan woman and Jesus happening today?

What does it mean to "truly" worship God?

Who is doing worship the right way?

Is the way you worship Biblical?

What kind of worship style do you have?

WORSHIP STYLE

I know some of my dearest friends think I'm way off but I believe the whole notion of "worship style" is an oxymoron. I'm not stuck in this so feel free to dialogue with me or others you know about this, but worship should be more about what you declare about God than about how you package it. When we describe worship in terms of what fits with our fashion, what are we really saying?

Consider how hairstyle, clothes, and entertainment have changed in the last hundred years.

Think about how life-style has changed in the last hundred years.

Think about how the style of human relationships changed over the last 100 years through the technological revolution.

When I look at people in the Bible, I don't see or hear a lot of discussion about personal style. The word worship occurs 188 times. Worshipped—69 times. Worshipper is mentioned in 9 different places. Worshipping, 5 times. And since these figures come from the King James Version, we need to be consistent—the word "worshippeth" turns up in the Bible 6 times. It took me a few weeks but I looked up every passage and added the word "worthy" in for good measure since it is related. As you would guess, the diversity of these aforementioned passages is great. Nevertheless, I noticed a trend in the Bible that four verbs seem to prelude much of the worship and all those who "worshippeth" God.

Come before God to worship

Serve and worship

Bowed your head in worship

Fall down and worship

From discussions to what it means to be "reverent" to holding firm to the need for "personal expression" in worship, I wonder if we could do better. Worship is what you say about God and to God. Style is how you describe what is preferable or characteristic of an individual.

"I need to feel comfortable when I worship God."

"I worship better when there is music I enjoy."

"I experience God's presence more when I…"

Many people choose churches because of worship "style." It is important for worship leaders to create the best environment for worship and remove as many distractions as possible; create every opportunity for God's presence to be experienced. But God can be avoided even under the most well constructed circumstances. You can sing a praise song solely because you like the way it sounds or out of habit and never give a thought to God as you sing.

Whether you worship in a coliseum or a church so small you double the attendance when you darken the doorway, "worship style" may be an unavoidable, inherent reality. But what is disturbing about the whole discussion is the primary focus on the needs of the worshipper rather than on the truth about the One who is being worshipped.

The praise song versus the 400 year old hymn.

The conversational preacher versus the more charismatic pulpit-pounding evangelist.

The big church experience versus the family room atmosphere.

Let's be honest—Our worship today has a lot to do with us. It's not that we don't all have our preferences for praising God—it's that we are willing to fight bitterly over our preferences in the very presence of the One who is Most Important.

When Jesus met with the Samaritan woman, they ended up in a conversation about the "how's" and "where's" of worship. Jesus brings the discussion of worship back to object of worship—Him:

The woman said, "I know that Messiah" (called Christ) "is coming. When he comes, he will explain everything to us." Then Jesus declared, "I who speak to you am he."

The Savior wanted the woman's heart—a converted heart that has embraced God's grace and desires to live in complete surrender and adoration of Him. The worshipper who worships in "spirit and in truth" worships from their heart to God—no matter what the circumstances are. Matt Redman's chorus says it well:

I'm coming back to the heart of worship, and it's all about You.

It's all about You Jesus.

I'm sorry, Lord, for the thing I've made it, when it's all about You.

It's all about You Jesus.

I still like my music. I'm even learning to love music I never dreamed I'd even understand. But let's be clear about style: it is a way to express myself. But not *the way*. Style changes, so will I, and so will you. Whether it be the sixteenth century or the twenty-first, each era has something to offer, and all eras have something to learn from one another. Worship is about what we choose to offer God. More often than not, the trends have everything to do with our styles—whether it be music, clothes or hair. You, on the other hand, have everything to say about Who is worshipped.

 As you approach God with a heart of worship—try telling Him what you want to say in ways you have not done before. It might be through a hymn, a prayer, or a letter.

As you reflect on the way you love to worship God, write about the difficulty of separating the way you love to worship and the One you are worshipping. Reflect on what you think God wants from you as to come to worship Him.

DAY 17 · ONE RETURNED TO GIVE PRAISE

"Now on his way to Jerusalem, Jesus traveled along the border between Samaria and Galilee. As he was going into a village, ten men who had leprosy met him. They stood at a distance and called out in a loud voice, "Jesus, Master, have pity on us!" When he saw them, he said, "Go, show yourselves to the priests." And as they went, they were cleansed. One of them, when he saw he was healed, came back, praising God in a loud voice. He threw himself at Jesus' feet and thanked him—and he was a Samaritan. Jesus asked, "Were not all ten cleansed? Where are the other nine? Has no one returned to give praise to God except this foreigner?" Then he said to him, "Rise and go; your faith has made you well." (Luke 17:11-19)

This story is loaded with rich insight, but one phrase strikes at the center of one of the most salient qualities in those who worship: vision. I'm not referring to the ability to appreciate aesthetics or mastering the art of leadership strategy, but the ability to "notice" the significant things that happen. One of the ten lepers healed "saw that he was healed." What was different about his attitude in comparison to the nine who did not see the same thing?

It seems that there is a "which came first, the chicken or the egg?" scenario here. There is a tension between what we see and our attitude about our experiences. Does our attitude shape how we see things? Or does our view of the world produce the attitude?

The conundrum reminds me of the story of a young boy in kindergarten who wanted to be in the school play. Of course, he would have to audition for a particular part and his mother so afraid he would be crushed if not chosen. The boy pleaded with his mom to let him try out. Not wanting to quench his adventurous spirit, she let her son try out for a part in the play. As the young boy's mother pulled up to the curb she was afraid that her son would be rejected but she was ready with words of comfort when her son rushed out through the doors with a smile beaming from his face. The boy jumped into the car looking straight into his mother eyes and said, "I got a part in the school play!" His mother inquired, "What part did you get, son?" With his eyes full of pride he announced, "I'm going to clap and cheer." Attitude enables you to see things differently.

In a similar way, attitude seems to be the "difference-maker." However, trying to change the way you think and feel about your experience is more difficult than it might seem. Imagine what the world would be like if people could easily just *change their attitude.*

As a teenager, I heard a phrase that I will probably hear myself repeat as my son is now a teenager. While the suggestions came in a variety of forms, the most common phrase I heard was, "Boy, you better curb that attitude." To call it a suggestion is a gross understatement—It was more of a threat. The problem was that it is next to impossible for a human to just switch their attitude into reverse.

I wanted to say:

"Father, with all due respect, are you asking me to reverse my emotional and cognitive position on the spot? Please understand that nothing could be more difficult. Think about what you are asking me to do. Imagine if that were possible, Dad. Racial hatred would be no more! Rapists and serial killers would take up golf and crochet instead of killing! There would be no need for political parties if someone could simply command an attitude adjustment."

The above response might have provoked more harm than resolution.

Like the leper who worshipped Jesus, something about his experience shaped his attitude in a way that caused him to see more than just healing from a disease. Two words are used in this story for healing. The first word refers to the ten lepers being "cleansed" or set free from the effects of the disease. But when the one returns and gives thanks, Jesus says, "Your faith has made you well," which means, *you have been saved*. Thinking about what God has done for you will shape your attitude, which will cause you to see things differently, which will foster new thoughts in your heart, which will transform your attitude, which will... You get the idea.

I used to be nervous around farmers. Tillers of the ground made me very uncomfortable for some reason. They never seemed to exude creative energy and whenever there was a problem farmers tended to retreat to "what works" as opposed to "what might work." The phrase, "I never had much use for that" was a common expression I'd hear farmers say to my creative suggestions. I never had much use for people raining on my creative party.

My attitude changed when I was assigned to a whole church full of farmers. I walked in the freshly tilled soil. I rode in a combine. I visited them in their cornfields. I listened to their insightful approach to living. I noticed how they kept the church out of debt even when their own finances were uncertain. I began to wonder, "How did they become so aware of the world around them?" I marveled at how keenly they could size up the sincerity of people. Real farmers freakishly know stuff.

My attitude about farmers changed because my experiences changed. When you walk up the steps to the church for worship, what experiences have you had this week that have given you an attitude of joy and praise? What have you seen?

If your attitude isn't right consider the following questions:

1. Do you actively seek opportunities to be a cup of cool water for someone?

2. Have you prayed for God to live in you and through you—and seized those moments during the week?

3. Have you spent time reflecting on your week about what God has done in you and around you? Sometimes on Friday night a whole wave of blessings can crash in on you after a busy week.

4. Have you thought about Creation, Calvary, or the Coming of the Lord Jesus Christ? Meditating on these three events alone is enough to turn your head around.

Before you enter into moments of worship this week consider what you think God has done and is doing in your life.

 Make a list today of the things you want to praise God for in church this week. Write them down and put them in your Bible throughout the week so that, during the service you can celebrate the great things God has done.

Reflect on the types of things you found yourself praising God for this week. What does your list say about you?

DAY 18 · WHO IS THIS?

 "That day when evening came, he said to his disciples, "Let us go over to the other side." Leaving the crowd behind, they took him along, just as he was, in the boat. There were also other boats with him. A furious squall came up, and the waves broke over the boat, so that it was nearly swamped. Jesus was in the stern, sleeping on a cushion. The disciples woke him and said to him, "Teacher, don't you care if we drown?" He got up, rebuked the wind and said to the waves, "Quiet! Be still!" Then the wind died down and it was completely calm. He said to his disciples, "Why are you so afraid? Do you still have no faith?" They were terrified and asked each other, "Who is this? Even the wind and the waves obey him!" (Mark 4:31-35)

 Worship. Circumstances teach us that "who" comes before "how". Why did they worship Jesus? There was the wind, the waves, the voice, the calm; then there was the worship. Matthew's version of the story claims, "those who were in the boat worshipped him." (Matt 14:23-36)

While worship is an attitude, it is often prompted by an event. Have you ever had a moment that became "an event" that brought you to the place of worship?

The story of Jesus calming the sea is an event that awakened worship in the disciples. Did they know who Jesus was? Surely Jesus had done this type of thing before. But the passage says they worshipped Him saying, "Truly you are the Son of God." Was there ever any doubt? Well, maybe, but maybe not. The disciples fell on their knees in worship because it dawned on them, again, who Jesus was. The fact that Jesus just walked on the water woke them up a bit.

Can you imagine the disciples breaking out into a discussion on whether they should kneel, sing or be silent at the moment of their rescue on the lake? Their discovery was in the nature and character of God at that moment: "They worshipped Him saying,

'Truly you are the Son of God.'"

In college, I did a project to see if a small crowd of people treated an unknown individual as though they were famous.

A group of suspiciously well-dressed students would walk through the mall surrounding a supposedly famous person wearing sunglasses. They would move through the mall with purpose, as though they were trying to avoid being mobbed. Several planted fans would come up to the poser asking for autographs, hoping to secretly incite a clamor of others to join in the fray.

The experiment yielded a few curious onlookers (mostly teenagers), but for the most part the pseudo-celebrity did not inspire awe or the adoration of the masses.

Maybe the superstar just didn't have the aura of fame. Maybe you really have to be special to get special treatment. Maybe the shoppers were so fixed on their business that coming face to face with a super star was not a convenient option.

Who is this King of glory? What does it mean to be standing before the Eternal God of love? What makes the moment of worship life-changing is coming face to face with God and recognizing Him for who He is. If you ponder for a moment what it means to be able to speak to the God who carved the earth with a few careful phrases and it's not going to be "Jesus as usual." No wonder the saints of old would cover their eyes, fall to their knees, and place their hands over their mouths.

 Ask God to give you reminders throughout the rest of the week to worship spontaneously. As the reminders appear, seize them and share those moments with your partner; or, plan moments of worship if you have a flexible schedule. Try going into your church when no one is there and it is quiet.

Reflect and write about the way God reveals Himself to you. Think about the times God arrested your attention with big events. Reflect on the smaller, more subtle ways God has tried to get your attention. Think about your responses in those moments and how you want to continue to respond in the future.

DAY 19 · I MUST STAY AT YOUR HOUSE

 "He entered Jericho and was passing through. And there was a man named Zacchaeus. He was a chief tax collector and was rich. And he was seeking to see who Jesus was, but on account of the crowd he could not, because he was small of stature. So he ran on ahead and climbed up into a sycamore tree to see him, for he was about to pass that way. And when Jesus came to the place, he looked up and said to him, "Zacchaeus, hurry and come down, for I must stay at your house today." So he hurried and came down and received him joyfully. And when they saw it, they all grumbled, "He has gone in to be the guest of a man who is a sinner." And Zacchaeus stood and said to the Lord, "Behold, Lord, the half of my goods I give to the poor. And if I have defrauded anyone of anything, I restore it fourfold." And Jesus said to him, "Today salvation has come to this house, since he also is a son of Abraham. For the Son of Man came to seek and to save the lost." (Luke 19:1-10, ESV)

 The phone rang several times before David answered cautiously. I mentioned I was in the area and wanted to stop by and see how he was doing. An awkward pause swallowed the next few seconds until he found something to say.

"To what do I owe the privilege of a pastoral visit?" he chuckled nervously. David was a joker and was always quick with his wits. But today there were no quick comebacks or dry jokes to be found. Over the course of the last few weeks, he wasn't laughing nor was he showing up to be his jovial self in the community at church.

"David, I missed you at church and I just wanted to check and see if you were alright. Would you mind if I dropped by?"

Again, several seconds of awful silence followed. Finally the tension was broken by a series of excuses just as I pulled up in front of his house. I waved to Dave who was looking out the front window with the phone to his ear looking back at me, frozen like a deer in the headlights. Hanging up he waved me inside.

"I guess I can't avoid you any longer." Several indicators confirmed my suspicions about the degree to which Dave felt far away from his church: The "for sale" sign on the grass, the empty garage, a solitary chair and a few boxes peppered the living room floor, the sleeping bag on the floor, fast food bags on the kitchen counter, and Dave holding his hands out in confession, "She's gone." Dave's wife had left him for greener pastures. A few days of dis-connection had formed a chasm like the Grand Canyon between Dave and his church family.

When it finally dawned on me that something was wrong, I went to his home. Home is where the heart is—even the broken ones. Home is where we are who we are and, in Dave's case, both he and his home were empty. His next few words were even more telling. "I was wondering if you were going to show up sooner or later." While "later" is better than "never," when help came, it came to where he lives—his house.

In the case of Zacchaeus, help came to his house and didn't make an appointment. Forgiveness and renewal came, not in the form of a card or an email, but in a person who showed up to eat at his house. While there are many assumptions people have about this little man, one seems to be that it was while Jesus ate with him that he experienced conversion. Luke uses the present tense when he has Zacchaeus saying, "Lord, the half of my goods **I give** to the poor. And if I have defrauded anyone of anything, **I restore** it fourfold." This means that the little fellow had already been living honorably, beyond the call of duty. Zacchaeus was hated by people in spite of his generosity!

Have you ever been that alone?

As close as you are to your friends there is always enough space between you for distance to grow. Dallas Willard describes the power of connectedness by saying:

Personalities united can contain more of God and sustain the force of his greater presence much better than scattered individuals. The fire of God kindles higher as the brands are heaped together and each is warmed by the other's flame. The members of the body must be in contact if they are to sustain and be sustained by each other.[7]

The gift of friendship is hard-wired deep inside each of us—we need to be with one another. As matter of fact, the phrase "one another" or "each other" is repeated many times in the New Testament. Look at just a few and see what you think:

"A new command I give you: Love one another. As I have loved you, so you must love one another." (John 13:34)

"Be devoted to one another in brotherly love. Honor one another above yourselves." (Romans 12:10)

"Accept one another, then, just as Christ accepted you, in order to bring praise to God." (Romans 15:7)

"I myself am convinced, my brothers, that you yourselves are full of goodness, complete in knowledge and competent to instruct one another." (Romans 15:14)

"Be completely humble and gentle; be patient, bearing with one another in love." (Ephesians 4:2)

C. Leslie Charles observes the ultimate value of the human connection as well as the tenuous nature of relationships in today's world:

"The stronger your connections, the deeper your compassion. But when you lose your compassion, you also lose your passion. When your passion fades, your emotional connectedness begins to fray."[8]

Perhaps this is why Jesus makes the public declaration, "Today, salvation has come to this house, since this man is also a son of Abraham." Jesus adopts this man who is so misunderstood back in the family. Who do you know that needs to be restored?

Make a visit to a friend you have not really connected with in a while. Include in your visit a conversation about your own struggle to stay connected to God. Before: What are some of your expectations? After: What happened and how did you see God working in this exercise?

DAY 20 · YOU ARE MY FRIENDS

"My command is this: Love each other as I have loved you. Greater love has no one than this, that he lay down his life for his friends. You are my friends if you do what I command. I no longer call you servants, because a servant does not know his master's business. Instead, I have called you friends, for everything that I learned from my Father I have made known to you. You did not choose me, but I chose you and appointed you to go and bear fruit—fruit that will last. Then the Father will give you whatever you ask in my name. This is my command: Love each other." (John 15:12-17)

In John 15, Jesus elevates the concept of fellowship and friendship high on the list of human relationships. Jesus identifies two aspects of friendship that emerge in this conversation: 1) Jesus places the highest value (life) on the value of a friend, and 2) Jesus expects His friends to abundantly grow.

The concept of friendship with God is not a new idea ushered in by the New Testament. God considered Abraham a "friend". (2 Chronicles 20:7) And clearly the way God revealed Himself to Moses was not a normal epiphany: "The LORD would speak to Moses face to face, as a man speaks with his friend…" (Exodus 33:11)

Several truths about friendship grow out of the interchange between Jesus and the disciples that are important to being friends with Christ. The command is commissioned with the example, "love as I have loved you." Our friendships are to be marked with the same initiative, deeds, attitudes and responses that are painted across the canvas of the gospels by Jesus toward his disciples. It is not like He is asking us to do what we haven't already seen Christ model. He has given us an example of friendship loaded with stories and simple behaviors that make the example clear.

In the body of Christ, we love one another not because we have natural affinity toward one another, but because we are called to a greater bond than simply "liking someone."

Not only is friendship core to Christ's discipleship plan, Jesus expects His friends to grow abundantly because of their relationship to Him. "I chose you and appointed you to go and bear fruit, fruit that will last." The relationship makes you better, much better. Not only is the fruit of this friendship real, it lasts.

As a child I watched the tangerine tree in my yard grow to monstrous proportions. Not only did our citrus tree grow in size, but it overwhelmed our family and friends with an astonishing crop of fruit. My pride for the tree swelled from season to season, so much so that I thought the magic of growing fruit trees was simply genetic. So, when I grew up and the time came for me to plant my own fruit trees in my very own backyard, I picked out a tangerine tree to repeat the success of my father. I did everything to the soil I was taught to do: Cultivate, fertilize, mulch, protect, pray. After planting the tree in the ground, I continued the rituals week after week. I spoke kindly and gently to the tree as I worked in the yard. On one occasion, I even sang to the tree. But the tree failed to grow.

My patience ran out and I began to scorn the tree. "Silly runt weed! What's the matter with you?" I chided the defenseless citrus sprout. "Every other tree in the yard is doing just fine. You are turning out to be such a disappointment!" I added. On another day I was raking some leaves in the yard near the base of the puny tangerine tree when the rake got tangled at the base of the tree. I reached down to unhook the prongs of the rake and discovered the tag of the tangerine tree was still attached. I glanced at the tag and to my horror I read, "Tangerine...(Dwarf)."

I tried to take back all the horrible things I had said. I looked at the little tree and apologized, "I'm so sorry! I didn't realize you were never meant to grow."

Not so with you and me. According to Christ, we are destined to change into His likeness. Consider the promise given by the Master Teacher:

"A student is not above his teacher, but everyone who is fully trained will be like his teacher". (Luke 6:40) We can grow. We should grow. And the growth we experience is meant to be more than a good feeling from a stirring revival sermon or the occasional chill down our spines at the climax of a well-performed power ballad.

Fruit-bearing disciples are not super saints, but they live bent toward a genuine walk with God. Their growth is the result of divine grace at work in their lives. Their lifestyle is marked by the exercises that strengthen the muscles of the soul and their souls are marked by the presence of the Holy Spirit.

Relationships have rules. The simple and unspoken rules of friendship appear mostly when the rules are broken. All friendships are ordered and defined by standards.

Jesus defined the rules of friendship with one word: Love. Love brings us together. Love keeps us working. Love is the reason and the rule of our behavior to one another in the body of Christ.

Many assume that good relationships take care of themselves, however, if you look at any of the relationships Christ had with His disciples, you will notice a progression of growth as well as intentional events that deepen their commitments to one another. In many ways, friendships are like building houses; it takes time and work to build and maintain them, but one stick of dynamite has the power to bring them down.

 Write a note or email to a friend and share what you feel God wants you to say. Consider the task of loving people the way Jesus commanded in the verse for today. Imagine what the church might be like if people were to take this command seriously.

DAY 21 · BEING SALT AND LIGHT—SEEING GOD

"You are the salt of the earth. But if the salt loses its saltiness, how can it be made salty again? It is no longer good for anything, except to be thrown out and trampled by men. "You are the light of the world. A city on a hill cannot be hidden. Neither do people light a lamp and put it under a bowl. Instead they put it on its stand, and it gives light to everyone in the house. In the same way, let your light shine before men, that they may see your good deeds and praise your Father in heaven." (Matthew 5:13-16)

In the passage above, Christ is calling for the disciples to attempt the old pick-and-roll. The pick-and-roll is a classic basketball play. Night in and night out future hall-of-famers John Stockton and Karl Malone of the Utah Jazz use the pick-and-roll to baffle defenses. The other teams know it's coming, but are usually helpless if the play is well executed.

The American Reference Dictionary describes the pick and roll as follows:

An offensive play in which a player stops to block a defender [the pick] for a teammate handling the ball and then slips behind the defender [the roll] to accept a pass.

The dynamic duo, John Stockton and Karl Malone, perfected the pick-and-roll. Their names are virtually inseparable. If basketball has a duet more closely knit together and necessary to each other's success than these two, it will be difficult to find. Steals and assists. Points scored over the long haul. Anyone who knows anything about professional basketball knows that Stockton and Malone did more together than they would have ever done alone. The two aren't hotshots. Neither of them alone were dominant basketball players. Karl Malone is not much bigger or stronger than most power-forwards and Stockton doesn't stand out as the most physically talented point guard on the court. What do these two have to do with Christ calling believers to be salt and light?

The "you" in the passage is plural—not singular. You—when you are together— are salt. No one would buy a sour cream potato chip—but sour cream and onion is a popular choice in grocery stores today. Together they belong and together they are appreciated. "Synergy" is another way to describe it.

Synergy essentially implies that the whole is greater than the sum of its parts. Jesus sends the disciples out two by two for a reason—synergy. They are better together than they would have been alone. Why? They remind each other of mission. They enable each other with courage. The disciples foster a sense of community, which creates a boldness that rarely exists when people feel alone.

I saw synergy in the shopping mall. A tremendously shy teenager in one of my classes sauntered down the center of the mall with her best friend, who was equally as shy. I couldn't believe what I saw—they were singing! Not humming quietly, but singing loudly obnoxiously some popular new song—in the middle of the mall. They appeared to be only a little embarrassed, but still enjoying the power of togetherness in a way that made me wonder if it was really them.

Personal or private. Some might say that our relationship with God is personal-meaning private. The believer can't quite choke out the word "private" because it contradicts what Christ commands us to be—quite public. In truth, a growing relationship with God will be personal (intimate between the individual and God) as well as public.

There is no question that each of us must relate personally to God. But God created us to be what I call, "pair-a-normal." Not the extra-terrestrial or X-File type, but rather the combination of two doing what one cannot. I'll step out on a limb here and make a statement; we simply don't grow spiritually by ourselves. People are better, deeper, braver, wiser, and flat out more effective as a team than they are alone. Most of us grow when we have a connection with others who desire the same thing.

Christ describes the promised result:

"In the same way, let your light shine before men, that they may see your good deeds and praise your Father in heaven."

God is glorified by your togetherness. In our disconnected world, the church is made stronger by our synergy.

Make a list of the dynamic duos in your life—the people who are famous to you because they demonstrate the quality of synergy—who are better together than separate. Do something this week with your partner in the journey that you would never do alone—for God, it could be a community service project, an act of kindness—whatever. Just do it together. Discuss how the dynamic of synergy exists in your relationships.

Make a meal with a friend or go out to eat with each other. Order something new or make something you have never made. The idea is to try something new that you can do together. Talk about something you have never had a conversation about. Devote yourself to this!

Reflect on some of the most meaningful events of your life and with whom you shared those moments. Pray and talk to God about the gifts He has given you in friends.

1 Patrick Kavanaugh, Worship—A Way of Life, (Grand Rapids, Michigan: Chosen Books, 2001), p. 23.

2 Dallas Willard, The Spirit of the Disciplines, (New York: HarperCollins, 1988), p. 177.

3 Richard Foster, Celebration of Discipline, (New York: HarperCollins, 1988), p.179.

4 International Standard Bible Encyclopaedia, Electronic Database Copyright (c)1996 by Biblesoft.

5 Peter V. Deison, Edited by Kenneth O. Gangel & James C. Wilhoit, The Christian Editor's Handbook On Spiritual Formation, (Grand Rapids, Michigan: Baker Books, 1994), p. 270.

6 Ibid, p.270.

7 Dallas Willard, The Spirit of the Disciplines, (New York: HarperCollins, 1988), p. 186.

8 C. Leslie Charles, Why Is Everyone So Cranky?, (New York: Hyperion Press, 2001), p. 124,125.

Small Group Questions—
WORSHIP AND FELLOWSHIP

If you were to define worship in one sentence, how would you communicate the experience as accurately as possible?

Describe a time of worship that was especially meaningful to you. What happened and how did it affect you? What were some of the components that contributed to the significance of the event?

What do you think is the relationship between corporate worship and private personal worship? Some think worship begins as a community and feeds the desire for personal worship, while others would reverse the process. What do you think?

If you were to design an hour of worship that would truly honor God in your community, what would it look like?

What are some attitudes and perceptions you have about worship that you think need to be changed?

What relationships in the church would you say have caused you to grow significantly? Name two or three and share why these people were so influential in your life.

Describe your church community and the dynamics of fellowship in the congregation. What would you affirm and what would you encourage them to change?

Can you think of a time when honesty in your friendships was difficult but the growth you experienced was worth the risk? How do members of the church body model honesty without offense? What is foundational to such experiences?

What are your strengths and weaknesses as a friend?
What can you do to be a better friend?

Share some of your thoughts on how to create a sense of connectedness among different generations.

—WEEK 4—
Confession and Secret Goodness

This week the exercise of confession will drive you to be public with your devotion while secrecy will challenge you to privately spend kindness on someone who will never thank or repay you. Reflect for a moment on some of the core ideas about the exercise of Christian confession and secret kindness.

Confession

The reality of how little we know about each other is a bit frightening. Broken relationships emerge before anyone can assemble help. Suicide. Abuse. Loneliness. Depression. Alienation. Apathy. Injustice. While our relationship with God is personal, it is also communal. When God said, "it is not good for man to be alone" He spoke beyond the suggestion of marriage to the idea that "two is better than one." In other words, God never meant for us to live out our spiritual lives in utter privacy. If there is a mountain to climb in the twenty first century church, it is the Mt. Everest of transparency and humility in the community of faith. For this we need the ancient exercise of confession.

Consider what some of the most respected authors of the spiritual growth say about confession in the community of faith:

"Confession is a discipline that functions within fellowship. In it we let trusted others know our deepest weaknesses and failures. This will nourish our faith in God's provision four our needs through his people, our sense of being loved, and our humility before our brothers and sisters."[1]

"The highest level of fellowship—involving humility, complete honesty, transparency, and at times confession and restitution—is sustained by the discipline of submission."[2]

The obsession to demand that things go the way we want them to go is one of the greatest bondages in human society today. People will spend weeks, months, even years in a perpetual stew because some little thing did not go as they wished."[3]

"To confess means to own up to the fact our behavior wasn't just the result of bad parenting, poor genes, jealous siblings, or a chemical imbalance from too many Twinkies. All of those factors may be involved. Human behavior is a complex thing. But confession means saying that somewhere in the mix was a choice, and the choice was made by us, and it does not need to be excused, explained, or even understood. The choice needs to be forgiven. The slate has to be wiped clean."[4]

Confession occurs with our relationship to God as well as our relationship with others. While it seems safer to be honest and open with God and quite unnerving to be the same with people, we can begin the process of change by becoming someone who is trustworthy, compassionate, and humble.

Secret Goodness

Publius Syrus once said, "You can accomplish by kindness what you cannot by force." The impact is magnified when acts of kindness are done in secrecy. Dallas Willard explains:

"Secrecy rightly practiced enables us to place our public relations department entirely in the hands of God, who lit our candles so we could be the light of the world, not so we could hide it under a bushel. We allow him to decide when our deeds will be known and when our light will be noticed."[5]

Secret goodness challenges you to serve someone else in such a way that you will not be rewarded—other than the satisfaction that you have put a smile of the face of God. For some, extending secret acts of kindness is the purest form of service possible. It may seem like secret goodness is fluffy compared to some of the other disciplines, but in reality, it taxes us as deep as we go—to our motivation. Some can offer service to others knowing they will be perceived as a generous, helpful person. However, when your acts of righteousness are done in secret, only God sees them. That alone is its' own special kind of reward.

DAY 22 · LIFT WITH CARE—NOT HEAVY

 "Come to me, all you who are weary and burdened, and I will give you rest. Take my yoke upon you and learn from me, for I am gentle and humble in heart, and you will find rest for your souls. For my yoke is easy and my burden is light." (Matthew 11:28-30)

 The drawing portrayed a young man carrying a boy on his back. The little one, with his arms locked around the front of the neck and his sleepy head leaned peacefully off to the side. The older boy's body is upright and his face is stretched in a broad smile. When Father Flanagan saw this picture, he added the caption: "He ain't heavy, he's my brother."

Father Edward Flanagan used this image to capture the purpose of his mission: To give neglected, homeless boys a place to grow, and perhaps take up another way of life. Flanagan's motto was: "There are no bad boys. There is only bad environment, bad training, bad example, bad thinking." So, with a $90 loan he placed his first five homeless boys in a rented house in Nebraska.

Later, Bobby Mills and Bob Scott wrote the song that The Holly's, Neil Diamond, and even Cher went on to make popular. Boy's Town is almost a hundred years old now and although it has recently endured a few dark seasons of scandal, its' purpose was to invite boys to take up another identity, and another way of life.

When Christ called to weary people He promised them rest. He invited people exhausted by the meaningless repetition of duties, religion, and hopeless endeavors to take up another "yoke." His yoke.

A yoke is a device to hold and steer a beast of burden. In a way, it is the tool that enslaves these animals to do work they are expected to do. Why trade one yoke for another? Jesus claimed that His yoke is *"easy"* but the word means "well-fitted." When a carpenter would make a yoke for a farmer he would first measure the animal carefully to craft a yoke that would rest properly on the ox. A well-made yoke would empower the animal instead of encumber the poor beast. As a craftsman, Jesus knew how to make a yoke that fit a beast properly. Moreover, as the Son of God, He knew that our devotion to Him as Savior and Lord would fit us better than any selfish endeavor this world would ever strap on our backs.

What does this have to do with the exercise of confession? Confession is to actively submit to the truth about who you are. But Christian confession implies more than admission of "who you are," but also conveys a desire to "be someone else."

If someone confesses to a crime they are stepping out from the pretense that they are innocent and admitting they are guilty. Sadly, this often occurs not because of a deep sense of sorrow or internal conviction, but results when all of the options for hiding, lying, and pretending are taken away by evidence.

When I was in the fifth grade I became addicted to taking things apart. I took apart anything electronic or motorized, from small household appliances to eight-track tape players (if you don't know what this is—google it). I was out of control. I honestly believed I could use the motor of a vacuum cleaner for a go-kart engine. The vacuum cleaner sounded so jet-like in contrast to go-karts, which back then, were only glorified lawnmowers. You might laugh, but I was dreadfully serious about finding a way to turn an appliance into a vehicle.

The answer hid somewhere behind the various layers of plates and screws. Deeper and deeper I made my way through the innards of the machine. Naturally, I became quite skilled at unscrewing things, but alas, I did not find a way to make a vacuum cleaner into a go-kart. What became just as evident was the fact that I had no idea how to turn the disassembled bucket of parts back into a vacuum cleaner again. So, I hid what was now a bucket of screws, wires, and unrecognizable parts behind our neighbor's shed and hoped that that my parents would never feel the urge to vacuum anything, ever again.

Sure enough, one day, (the same day my parents felt the urge to vacuum something) Mr. Rob was cleaning behind his shed. I stood before my parents who held in their hands what used to be our vacuum cleaner. At first I lied and then I tried to explain, but finally I confessed.

Confession is both scary and liberating. Yet, the most human thing to do is to respond to guilt with a defense, or shame with a lie, or weakness with self-reliance. Jesus offers an invitation: *The work of being a child of God is work, but it fits you well—so well you will sweat with joy and press forward with peace and produce a life abundant with meaning because your identity finally fits the frame you were created for.*

When I hear Jesus say, "Come to me all who are weary" and "I will give you rest," He is urging them to put away a life of emptiness and take up a life that is full. To do this, one must admit that both the emptiness we are in and the abundance we hope for are real.

Maybe, Jesus is not offering a new identity, but inviting people to return to the one they were created for.

 Think about all the things you have that fit well. Consider also the things that you own that don't fit well. Some of the things that fit well do so because you wore them enough and some things will never be comfortable no matter how much you wear them. Apply this day's passage to the things you see, sit in, put on, and play in. Perhaps you could put some clothes on that simply fit well today to remind you to be true to your calling. Or, perhaps there are things you want to remind yourself of that don't fit in your life that you want to confess to God, "These things don't fit your plan for me." Some may want to wear the awkward, ill-fitting stuff as a symbol of their confession that there is something better.

Take the time to reflect on the things that fit and the things that don't in light of Christ's calling in your life.

DAY 23 · THE BIGGEST THREE LETTER WORD

 "When he had finished speaking, he said to Simon, "Put out into deep water, and let down the nets for a catch." Simon answered, "Master, we've worked hard all night and haven't caught anything. But because you say so, I will let down the nets." When they had done so, they caught such a large number of fish that their nets began to break. So they signaled their partners in the other boat to come and help them, and they came and filled both boats so full that they began to sink. When Simon Peter saw this, he fell at Jesus' knees and said, "Go away from me, Lord; I am a sinful man!" (Luke 5:3-8)

 Waterskiing didn't look complicated. "How hard can it really be?" I thought to myself as the group of girls asked me if I knew how to waterski and whether I would like to go.

I agreed, pretending to know how to waterski. Although I had never been on skis I avoided that bit information and replaced it with a bold-faced lie. I only have myself to blame for what happened next. After minutes of wriggling in the water, I finally got the skis on, bent my knees, straightened my arms, and nodded my head. Sure enough, I popped straight up on the skis and I was skiing for the first time. It was easy.

After six seconds of glory both skis flipped off and I fell, but I failed to let go of the rope. After I lost my swimming trunks in the water, I let go of the rope. When the boat drew closer I called for a towel because I was covered with only my life jacket, and shame. I became aware of who I was, and who I was not on the lake that day.

On another lake Peter thought he knew what he was doing too; he was an expert fisherman. He knew there were no fish available for business in the afternoon. Nevertheless, the biggest three-letter-word in the world is "but." It is a watershed word. It is the continental divide separating ideas. "But" shows an unanticipated change of direction. Peter's words to Jesus are the watershed moment of confession: "Master, we've worked hard all night and haven't caught anything. But because you say so, I will let down the nets.

Notice some others who worked that three-letter word into their lives:

When you feel misunderstood and no one seems to be listening...

"Joseph's master took him and put him in prison, the place where the king's prisoners were confined. **But** while Joseph was there in the prison, the LORD was with him; he showed him kindness and granted him favor in the eyes of the prison warden." (Genesis 39:20-21)

When you want to preoccupy yourself with your rights and demand justice...

"May the arrogant be put to shame for wronging me without cause; **but** I will meditate on your precepts." (Psalms 119:78)

When you are frozen with fear...

"The wicked are waiting to destroy me, **but** I will ponder your statutes." (Psalms 119:95)

When you are not sure what God will do...

"Shadrach, Meshach and Abednego replied to the king, "O Nebuchadnezzar, we do not need to defend ourselves before you in this matter. If we are thrown into the blazing furnace, the God we serve is able to save us from it, and he will rescue us from your hand, O king. **But** even if he does not, we want you to know, O king, that we will not serve your gods or worship the image of gold you have set up." (Daniel 3:16-18)

When your resources don't seem to be enough...

"Then Peter said, 'Silver or gold I do not have, **but** what I have I give you. In the name of Jesus Christ of Nazareth, walk.'" (Acts 3:6)

When being faithful will surely bring uncertainty...

"Then they called them in again and commanded them not to speak or teach at all in the name of Jesus. **But** Peter and John replied, 'Judge for yourselves whether it is right in God's sight to obey you rather than God. For we cannot help speaking about what we have seen and heard.'" (Acts 4:18-20)

When you seem to be alone...

"So Peter was kept in prison, **but** the church was earnestly praying to God for him." (Acts 12:5)

The three letter word "but" may be one of the biggest words in the Bible. In this story Peter gets a glimpse as to "Who Jesus is" but also a clear sense as to who he is. Much like the reality that became clear to King Canute.

Canute was a Danish king who ruled England from 1016 to 1035. Tradition has it that Canute had a clear sense about who He was and who God was. Even though his subjects would offer him nothing but endless praise, he resisted. All the fussing and flattery annoyed him until one day, he took the entire court down to coast of Northampton and ordered that his thrown be set down in the sand. As the tide came in, Canute asked his advisors, "Do you think I am the mightiest king of all?" "Yes, your majesty, they replied." Canute continued, "Do you believe that I am the most powerful king of all?" The king's staff nodded and professed shamelessly, "Oh, yes, your majesty. You are the most powerful King of all." Canute inquired, "Do you think I am strong enough to stop the tide?" The staff answered with some uncertainty, "Yes, your majesty."

Standing up from his throne he roared at the oncoming tide, "Stop. I Canute, the ruler of England command you to come no further!" He continued to yell at the tide as his staff hung their heads clearly uncomfortable with their king's behavior. As the waves engulfed them all King Canute stood before his court staff soaking wet and stated, "It appears that the waves do not obey me. There is only one Lord over the land and sea—one God of the universe. Give your praise to Him alone." Soaked to the skin they marched back and Canute hung his crown in the church and never wore it again as a symbol that England's king gave allegiance to the King of Kings.

Think of an area of your life where you keep God at arms length. If you can't think of any, think harder. To a certain degree, we all struggle with surrender, but the work of confession is often among those most difficult to practice. Try it.

Reflect on the story on the lakeshore. Consider the outcome of Peter's confession to Christ. Meditate on the struggle Peter endured and examine your life and see if you have any scenarios that call for you to launch out into the deep.

DAY 24 · MY CONFESSION

"When Jesus came to the region of Caesarea Philippi, he asked his disciples…, "Who do you say I am?" Simon Peter answered, "You are the Christ, the Son of the living God." Jesus replied, "Blessed are you, Simon son of Jonah, for this was not revealed to you by man, but by my Father in heaven. And I tell you that you are Peter, and on this rock I will build my church, and the gates of Hades will not overcome it. I will give you the keys of the kingdom of heaven; whatever you bind on earth will be bound in heaven, and whatever you loose on earth will be loosed in heaven." (Matthew 16:13-19)

What a person thinks about Christ is the foundation of a relationship with Him. A.W. Tozer once said, "We tend by a secret law of the soul to move toward our mental image of God." What you are willing to confess—or say about Christ grows out of what you think of Him.

Jesus asked the disciples, "Who do you say I am?" Who do you think had a response? Before we package Peter up as a bull-headed big mouth we should recognize that he asked more questions than all the other disciples combined:

Peter asked Jesus to explain some of His hard sayings. (Matthew 15:15/ Luke 12:41)

Peter inquired how often he needed to forgive others. (Matthew 18:21)

Peter wondered about the reward the disciples would get for leaving everything behind. (Matthew 19:27)

Peter asked what the withering fig tree meant. (Mark 11:21)

Peter breaks the silence and confesses, "You are the Christ, Son of the Living God."

It is not enough to form an opinion about Christ. When you step forward and speak an answer, you become a witness. Jesus made it plain that the very structure of God's church is not built on footings or foundations made of stone, but on the solid convictions and rock hard beliefs of those who will confess Him.

Jesus called for a witness to confess what He believed. I needed such a witness when I was in a car accident many years ago.

The accident occurred when an oncoming car swerved into my lane and smashed my economy-sized car head on, bouncing me deep into the juniper bushes. Imagine a kindergartener colliding with a 250-pound linebacker. That linebacker was an 89 year-old woman attempting a left hand turn as I (kindergartner), inconveniently thwarted her efforts by being in her way. The story becomes even more surreal when the little old lady that jousted me off the road immediately left the scene, on foot, and made her way to the bank. Unbelievable.

The policeman asked, "Where is the other driver?" When I told him, "I think she went to the bank" he almost administered a sobriety test on me. After a few minutes she exited the bank and underwent a thorough examination by the paramedics and the police. Her words almost caused me to come unglued. "I was just turning to go into the bank and all of a sudden this car crashed into me." Unbelievable!

The officer re-interviewed me because it became my word stacked against the innocent demeanor of a sweet, 89 year-old lady. When I began explain again what *really* happened a young man walked over from the emergency vehicles and confessed to the policeman, "I saw the accident..." His testimony saved me. He saw the crash and decided to say what he knew.

It is not enough to see and know. You must be willing to declare your confession. But don't wait until you know everything! Peter didn't. When Peter makes his confession, what does he really know about Christ? His words are profound, but what did he mean by them? Although Peter courageously announces who he thought Jesus was, you can tell he was missing a few important points

First of all, **Peter doesn't fully understand Jesus' ultimate purpose.** Not long after this declaration Jesus describes his upcoming demise: "He then began to teach them that the Son of Man must suffer...and that he must be killed and after three days rise again." Peter could not stomach the Messiah going down like that so he rebuked Jesus for talking about dying. Jesus said to Peter, "Get behind me Satan..." Ouch!

Secondly, **Peter doesn't get how duplicitous his own heart is.** When Jesus warns Peter that he will deny the Lord three times, Peter claims, "I will never deny you. I will die for you." Part of our humanness dreams the unimaginable greatness we can achieve as well as admitting the betrayal we are capable of. The selflessness and selfishness are in us. Peter overestimated his devotion.

Third, **Peter doesn't fully get the mission of the church.** Even though Peter experienced the power of the Holy Spirit at Pentecost, he did not understand what it meant to be the church. Galatians 2:11-14 tells how Peter is still under a steep learning curve about who is "the church."

So here is our little rock of a disciple still struggling with the meaning of the gospel story Christ started in him years before.

Although Peter did not fully know, he believed. He did not completely understand this thing called church—but he embraced it. Jesus embraced Peter's short-sighted and shallow faith for what it truly was—a start. Christ honored Peter by saying, "God revealed this to you Peter, when people confess me to the world, nothing—not even the gates of hell will overcome it."

So, two thousand years later here we are. And church begins with what we say about who Christ is and what He has done for us. Even if our data is somewhat skewed or our emphasis is off a bit, we must come to a point of confession—say what you are thinking.

Who do you think I am? Describe the characteristics of God in a list of ten words or short phrases. Rank them in the order of importance, 1 being most important and 10 being least. As you look at the list, what does it tell you about your concept of God? What seems to be most important to you about the Person of God?

Consider how our understanding of a person's character affects the way we relate to them. Reflect on how this principle is true with people you relate differently to because of what you know about them. Reflect on how this is also true with God.

DAY 25 · WHEN IN DOUBT—KNOW DOUBT

"A man in the crowd answered, "Teacher, I brought you my son, who is possessed by a spirit that has robbed him of speech. Whenever it seizes him, it throws him to the ground. He foams at the mouth, gnashes his teeth and becomes rigid. I asked your disciples to drive out the spirit, but they could not." "O unbelieving generation," Jesus replied, "how long shall I stay with you? How long shall I put up with you? Bring the boy to me." So they brought him. When the spirit saw Jesus, it immediately threw the boy into a convulsion. He fell to the ground and rolled around, foaming at the mouth. Jesus asked the boy's father, "How long has he been like this?" "From childhood," he answered. "It has often thrown him into fire or water to kill him. But if you can do anything, take pity on us and help us." "'If you can'?" said Jesus. "Everything is possible for him who believes." Immediately the boy's father exclaimed, "I do believe; Help me overcome my unbelief!"" (Mark 9:15-25)

The poor man in the story is caught between his meager faith and desperate need to relieve his son from affliction. The faith that might make healing happen is just out of reach for the father but, instead of walking away the dad admits the truth: he is a little short on faith and needs help. Is that allowed?

Phillip Yancey comments on a similar scenario when many of Christ's disciples bolted and Jesus asks the doubt washed and uncertain few that remained, "You don't want to leave too, do you?" Their answer is not a striking proclamation of heroic faith. Frankly, their response is a bit weak. The disciples reply, "Lord, to whom shall we go? You have the words of life." It is a statement of faith, but also reflects a spectrum of unknowns Yancey admits subscribing to:

"That, for me, is the bottom-line answer to why I stick around. To my shame, I admit that one of the strongest reasons I stay in the fold is the lack of good alternatives, many of which I have tried. Lord, to whom shall I go? The only thing more difficult than having a relationship with an invisible God is having no such relationship."[6]

I want to thank Philip Yancey for saying so honestly what makes many Christians feel anxious and unsettled. In the church, and in our relationships with God, we need to begin with where we are instead of a standardized starting line of belief.

The tension between doubt and faith tends to make some uncomfortable. Wondering whether God exists or musing about the nature of His involvement in our lives is usually not a recommended mental exercise because of the potential damage it could do to one's "faith." Have you ever wondered if this "faith" thing is really worth it? Why not simply live according to what you can know for sure?

Some of my college students formed a list of questions they struggled with in their most transparent moments. Here is a short list—you may add your own questions if you like:

How much does God really want from us anyway?

Does the absence of our doubt somehow make miracles happen more often?

Does God ask us to leap mindlessly out in faith expecting miracles—as if by our action we move God to do something he would not otherwise do?

How much faith is really needed?

How do you quantify faith?

How do you know when you have "enough faith?"

Such questions survey the limits of our understanding. Obviously, the anonymous father in Mark 9 wrestled with his capacity to believe. Both faith and doubt are placed before the Savior as an offering and an admission. What is left to say or do when you put all your cards on the table? All that remains is absolute transparency. This is the beginning place of genuine confession. The fact that we take that unbelief and surrender it to God is the ultimate picture of faith.

Again, imagine the story where the man brings his demon-possessed boy to the disciples for healing. Christ had already given them authority over the unclean spirits, so this little tiff with the Devil should be a "no-contest" for the Lord's right hand disciples—right? Peter dramatically strikes out. James takes a swing and misses. John the beloved whiffs at making a miracle happen. What's up with trifecta of top-tier disciples? Is the magic gone? I can even hear James whisper, "Go around the circle and check for un-confessed sins!"

Their faith isn't enough but the honest confession of a desperate father is, "Tried… but they could not." Mel Lawrence paraphrases what seems to be the heart cry of the father:

"With as much as I know and as much as I have experienced and as much evidence as I have, I know that God is real, and He is good, and He is powerful, and He is here. I believe God knows; I believe God acts. But…there is so much I think I should believe that is beyond my reach and beyond my trust. My faith gets me just so far. I'm afraid if I go too far out on a limb, it will just break off. I fear that my desire to believe things that would be wonderful are just wishful thinking on my part. And I don't want to look like a fool. I don't want to be taken in. If I believe in and worship God, I want to know this God is real. So God, in all honesty, this is me: I do believe, and I think there is more I should believe but I have not been able to believe. Help me. I want to believe."[7]

It is enough, for now.

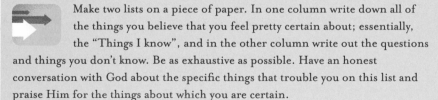

Make two lists on a piece of paper. In one column write down all of the things you believe that you feel pretty certain about; essentially, the "Things I know", and in the other column write out the questions and things you don't know. Be as exhaustive as possible. Have an honest conversation with God about the specific things that trouble you on this list and praise Him for the things about which you are certain.

Share the list with your partner. Reflect on the activity of making the two lists—what I know and what I don't know. Why do you think it is healthy to reflect on these things?

DAY 26 · TO BE OR NOT TO BE...SEEN

 "Be careful not to do your "acts of righteousness" before men, to be seen by them. If you do, you will have no reward from your Father in heaven. So when you give to the needy, do not announce it with trumpets, as the hypocrites do in the synagogues and on the streets, to be honored by men. I tell you the truth, they have received their reward in full. But when you give to the needy, do not let your left hand know what your right hand is doing, so that your giving may be in secret. Then your Father, who sees what is done in secret, will reward you." (Matthew 6:1-4)

 I was praising God when I received an "almost" anonymous gift. As I opened the card a hundred dollar bill fell to the floor. I picked it up and practically choked. Times were tight in college and every penny counted. The card came in the mail and I had no idea who sent it. It was a gift of the purist form because the giver chose to keep their identity a secret—until I arrived at church.

I was sitting in church thinking, "Who could have done this?" The answer came when the deacon asked for praises and thanksgiving, which was a bit unusual because he normally asked for only prayer requests.

He peered at me, "Does anyone have anything they are thankful for this week?" Not taking his eyes off me, he seemed to be patiently waiting for my response while other hands were practically waving in the air. I began thinking, "Mr. Deacon gave me the hundred bucks!" It was too obvious. I froze. He began to pick other people to share but always looked back at me.

"It has to be him," I thought. When everyone had exhausted their gratefulness he gave a final and more specific appeal, "Is there anyone who would like to share how God has surprised them with His grace this week?" He couldn't be more obvious. What bothered me the most was how he desperately tried not to keep his gift a secret.

At first I was grateful, but that joy moved to embarrassment. I stifled my thanksgiving out of rebellion. I wanted to raise my hand and say, "I'm grateful because someone sent us a hundred bucks this week but, we really needed two hundred." My wife made sure I did not speak up.

What reward do you seek in serving others? It is certainly not a sin when people know you have been kind to them. The point that Christ makes is that we should not seek recognition for our good deeds. When our kindness is given with no strings attached, our good deeds seem even greater.

Some keys to developing the discipline of secret goodness are:

Be kind to someone else in a way that glorifies God and not you.

When you extend kindness to someone secretly, be mindful of what God thinks rather than what others might say.

Take time to plan your service because secrecy sometimes requires extra work.

The story is told about a famous German artist named Herkomer, born in the Black Forest, whose father was a simple woodchopper. Herkomer was a gifted artist, and as his reputation grew he moved to London and built a studio there. He sent for his aged father, who came and lived with him, full of pride for his son.

The old man enjoyed creating things out of clay, and learned to make very beautiful bowls and vases. The father and son were in business together as artisans. But as the years passed, the old man's abilities deteriorated, and at the end of each day, as he went upstairs, he would seem sad because he felt that his work was now inferior to his son's.

Herkomer's sharp eye detected this, and when his father was safely upstairs and asleep for the night, Herkomer would come downstairs and take in his hand the pieces of clay that his father had left. He would gently correct the defects and the faults, and mold them as needed. When the old man would come down in the mornings, he would hold up the pieces in the morning light, smile, and say, "I can still do it as well as I ever did."

The smile of God is the sole reward and absolute treasure for disciples who practice secret goodness. The primary value of being secretive is to make God's glory central. Again, anyone can "do service projects" for others, but those who give tangible grace to others in secret deny themselves the accolades for the greater joy of feeling the smile of God.

As you undertake activities that only you and the Savior watching are aware of—it exposes the true beauty of service—your main goal is the joy of giving. The recognition from people is often nice, but doing the right thing for God's eyes only is the truest service of all.

Make a short list of secret acts of kindness you want to do throughout the week. Have it close by with you so you can cross the items off as you go.

For your journal experience, write one word at a time—single words that describe your experience practicing the discipline of secret goodness.

In which area of your life do you fail to see the forest because of the trees? As you do another act of kindness today, make a point to stop and ruminate about the big picture. Connect the simple act of kindness to the grand scheme of things and thank God for the chance to serve and for His smile. This is a way to connect the parts to the whole. Discover what works for you and practice stepping back and reflecting as you secretly give.

In which aspect of your spiritual journey can you say God "knows you" in the way mention in this lesson?

DAY 27 · ANDREW WHO?

 "Andrew, Simon Peter's brother, was one of the two who heard what John had said and who had followed Jesus. The first thing Andrew did was to find his brother Simon and tell him, "We have found the Messiah" (that is, the Christ). And he brought him to Jesus. Jesus looked at him and said, "You are Simon son of John. You will be called Cephas" (which, when translated, is Peter)." (John 1:40-42) Another of his disciples, Andrew, Simon Peter's brother, spoke up, "Here is a boy with five small barley loaves and two small fish, but how far will they go among so many?" (John 6:8-9) "Now there were some Greeks among those who went up to worship at the Feast. They came to Philip, who was from Bethsaida in Galilee, with a request. "Sir," they said, "we would like to see Jesus." Philip went to tell Andrew; Andrew and Philip in turn told Jesus." (John 12:20-22)

ANOTHER ANDREW

 It's not that Andrew is wealthy—he just has a big heart for people. Not only is he generous, he is downright sneaky. If he is at a restaurant, he will scan the place for a candidate to bless with a bit of kindness, secretly. One time it was dessert for a couple who seemed to be exhausted at the end of a busy week. Another time it was cookies to a table where a big family had gathered for a birthday celebration. Andrew always puts as much care into being anonymous as he puts into the gift.

One day, Andrew was filling his car up with gas and watching a frazzled mom trying to fill up her tank and keep her kids in line at the same time. He finished pumping his gas well before the woman and paid for both his fuel and hers without the struggling mom knowing. He pulled away from the gas station full of joy. He couldn't help himself!

I know Andrew—he isn't wealthy. He often struggles to make ends meet. But he seems to hear a different voice than many. He has eyes for people who need help and the reward he gains is a child-like joy that puts a smile on his face. I think God is smiling with him. Maybe Andrew is more wealthy than we originally thought.

It is one thing to not want credit for acts of kindness, it is an entirely different issue when you go out of your way to be unnoticed. At the heart of a secret deed of kindness is the reality that God alone will be glorified. Nobody becomes more esteemed, no one is more appreciated, respected or admired for their thoughtfulness.

Andrew (Both of them) reminds me of the kind of person who sneaks into a problem and leaves a solution as he sneaks out the back door, seemingly unnoticed. Andrew who? You remember Peter—How could you forget Peter? Who doesn't let an opportunity pass without announcing his official opinion, suggestion, or action-first-think-later approach to life. We know Peter, but what about his brother Andrew? Andrew is only mentioned in three stories in the Bible and in every scene, he does one thing—and only one thing. See if you can see a pattern in the above stories.

What Andrew does faithfully may not seem obvious—but his impact is real. Every time Andrew is mentioned, he is bringing someone to Jesus. He connects seekers to the Source of grace. Andrew is the one who brings Peter to Christ. Remember the boy with the loaves and fishes? Andrew walks him right up to the Savior. Then came the Greeks with heaps of difficult questions—Andrew leads them to the Master. Andrew is a connector. Subtle. Out of the way. Absolutely necessary. If secret goodness is about doing good and not being interested in getting credit, Andrew is our poster boy.

Ultimately, secret goodness is having as our only reward the Father saying, "Well done."

This discipline is going to challenge your spiritual muscle. On the surface, it sounds kind of fun—in reality, it is much more than giving trinkets or little bundles of kindness. This discipline simply seeks to please the Father. On this day in the desert try to remember the goal: Only God sees my service. Only God gets the glory.

By the way, whoever is responsible for the acts of kindness that come my way, I could thank you for it—but you already have your reward.

Think of two or three things you can do today that will please God but not identify you as the agent at work. It could be a note, an act of kindness, or simply an attitude like Andrew—just doing what needs to be done and getting out of the way.

How did this activity affect the intimacy you have with God? Think about how you felt throughout the day—especially during the moments of your secret service. What do you need to work on, focus on, surrender or commit to God?

DAY 28 · BECAUSE OF THE GIRLS

"After this, Jesus traveled about from one town and village to another, proclaiming the good news of the kingdom of God. The Twelve were with him, and also some women who had been cured of evil spirits and diseases: Mary (called Magdalene) from whom seven demons had come out; Joanna the wife of Cuza, the manager of Herod's household; Susanna; and many others. These women were helping to support them out of their own means." (Luke 8:1-3)

Did you catch the unsung squad of supporters that only Luke dared to mention? The women? The ministry of Jesus was bank rolled by "the girls." The nature of secret goodness is based on the fact that you don't seek public recognition. Luke is the only writer who mentions the breadwinners for the ministry of Jesus. We don't hear them screaming, "We want a piece of the pie. Come on boys—step up and chip in!" The ladies continue to support the ministry of Christ and don't say a word.

Maybe the girls could dedicate the tree where the Sermon on the Mount was given and place a placard with the names of "those who made this moment possible by their generous gift." I don't think they did and I'm glad. The girls received their reward—not the brief commercial in Luke, but they continue to foster the ministry of Christ. Who knows what the expenses entailed or where they got the money? Luke doesn't mention if they are rich or poor, only that they support the ministry.

If you want to know who these women are, you can look their names up in a concordance or Bible dictionary and get a better idea of what these girls are all about. But the essence of secret goodness is not to give you a window into the heart of the giver. It's not supposed to be about the giver at all. You might be curious enough to do a character sketch of these ladies, and if you do, you will find their stories reach all the way into the New Testament church. But they never ask for recognition, nor do they give in a way that others take notice. Their quiet legacy continues.

In Africa you notice them by their uniforms. Simple royal blue and white dresses are the standard uniform for the Dorcas ministry. The Dorcas Society is a group of volunteers who devote themselves to orphaned children, hungry families, and the sick and struggling. While I was holding some meetings in Zambia, I went visiting from door to door. Just as I walked up to a house, a woman in a blue dress walked out from the back of the house, glanced at me with a broad grin, and quickly went on her way. It seemed a little suspicious.

When the family came to the door, I went inside to visit. Just as we were about to pray, two children burst in from the back of the house holding shoes in their hands and what appeared to be school uniforms. "Someone left these on our back porch!" the mother translated. Tears were in her eyes as she explained, "We did not have enough money for the children's school clothes this year and someone..." She looked at me searching my face for any evidence that I was the one who had given the gift. "Oh no. I did not give those to you. I think it was..." I stopped. If the secret giver wanted to be known, she could have made it known.

Someone may mention your name in connection with acts of kindness. You can't always be elusive. The secret giver in the story above couldn't wipe the smirk of joy off her face after leaving the gift. Wouldn't it be exciting if the identifying mark of true believers were the smirks beaming on their faces from the irrepressible joy that comes from giving? But you will be noticed, but the question is, who will be glorified? Remember the words of Christ:

"Let your light shine before others, that they may see your good deeds and glorify your Father in heaven." (Matthew 5:16)

The women mentioned by Luke are not very well known to us today. Mary Magdalene is mentioned a few times in the Gospels and Joanna was a witness to the resurrection. (Luke 24:10) The identity of her husband, Cuza, and Susanna, and the "many other women" who supported Jesus remain undisclosed. In Luke's day they must have been well-known people of financial means who had left their husbands and families in order to underwrite a sizeable group of itinerate evangelists. Perhaps they were some of those first believers who sold their lands and houses and used the money to support the Jesus movement. (Acts 4:34) Perhaps their generosity was well known, but also well understood— like Arnold Billie.

Arnold is a mail carrier who lives and works out in the rural area of Southern New Jersey. His mail route covers over sixty-three miles through two counties and many small towns. Surprisingly, the mail is not all he delivers. Arnold Billie is both subtle and famous for his servant heart. The red flag on mailboxes usually indicates that there is mail to pick, but on Arnie's route it means, "I need help with something." Starting rusty old lawnmowers, moving furniture, holding the dog still for a bath—if you need a hand, postman Billie is willing if he is able. It is common knowledge to the locals, but others driving by see the red flags and may think, "Outgoing mail," but those who know thank God for people like Arnold Billie.

Try writing a letter to someone in the congregation that will encourage and honor their service. Pick someone you feel you can pour out a blessing of kindness on—and don't forget to mail it.

Reflect on the gift of praise and encouragement. When have you received words that had a lasting effect in your life? Consider how the menial process of writing a letter or sending a card is a timeless discipline.

1 Dallas Willard, The Spirit of the Disciplines, (New York: HarperCollins, 1988), p. 187.

2 Ibid, p. 189.

3 Richard Foster, Celebration of Discipline, (New York: HarperCollins, 1988), p.III.

4 John Ortberg, The Life You've Always Wanted, (Grand Rapids, Michigan: Zondervan, 1997), p. 124.

5 Dallas Willard, The Spirit of the Disciplines, (New York: HarperCollins, 1988), p. 172.

6 Philip Yancey, Reaching For The Invisible God, (Grand Rapids, Michigan: Zondervan, 2000), p.38.

7 Mel Lawrenz, I Want To Believe, (Ventura, California: Regal, From Gospel Light, 2007), p.13,14.

Small Group Questions—
CONFESSION AND SECRET GOODNESS

Share with each other some of the areas of life that are difficult to submit to Christ.

Imagine a church that understands and practices the discipline of confession as a way of life. What kinds of benefits would be realized? What are some potential pitfalls?

Who do you know in the church who seems like a person you could trust if you needed someone to pray with and to help you with a problem? What qualities does that person have that you would love to have as your own?

If you were to rank how well you think people really know each other in the church from 1 to 5—1 being close-knit and 5 being distant—how would you score your church?

Do you believe that the exercise of confession and submission are downplayed or emphasized? Why do you think this might be?

Share a time in your life when an act of secret kindness came your way. How did you feel? How did you respond?

Compare this discipline with the others you have been working on. How much does secret goodness require from you? Is this discipline more demanding for you than Bible study or Worship?

Imagine specific acts of kindness that would be helpful for others. Can you think of things that you could do anonymously to benefit the recipient.

How do you see this discipline working in the church, the community or the workplace?

Sabbath and Storytelling

Sabbath

There are some that would hesitate to include the Sabbath as an exercise but there is a danger in thinking about the Sabbath solely as a doctrinal truth. Everything about the word "Sabbath" screams, "STOP!" Sabbath is experiential. You can't understand it, preach it, defend it, illustrate it, or take a stand on it with any kind of meaning until you practice "stopping." The command from God is to remember to keep it. God cautioned people to "remember" a particular day for a reason—He knew we would be inclined to forget. And if we forgot to keep Sabbath, we would ultimately forget about our relationship to God.

"But **remember** the LORD your God, for it is he who gives you the ability to produce wealth, and so confirms his covenant, which he swore to your ancestors, as it is today." (Deuteronomy 8:18)

"**Remember** that you were slaves in Egypt and the LORD your God redeemed you." (Deuteronomy 15:15)

"**Remember** your Creator in the days of your youth." (Ecclesiastes 12:1)

Remember how God pricked the hearts of His people when they had utterly forgotten the relationship to the Creator. (Micah 6:1-8) Even though they were convicted of their forgetfulness they had forgotten God's character so completely that their first response was to sacrifice their children as part of their repentance. Forgetting is deadly.

Even the Israelites, not long after their deliverance grew impatient and forgot who God was and what He had done, so they urged Aaron to make a god out of gold. (Exodus 32) They did two things that illustrate how easily people can forget, and how detestable their sin can become: 1) They attributed to a golden cow the work of redemption, saying "This is our god who delivered us," 2) The memorialized that falsehood by proclaiming, "Tomorrow will be a festival to the Lord." You make a god and you make a day to worship it. How God's heart must have been broken.

Throughout Scripture, the Sabbath is that gift that connects us to God as our Creator (Exodus 20:8-11) and our Redeemer. (Deuteronomy 5:12-15) It is that sign that screams to the whole world that we belong to God. (Ezekiel 20:12,20) Since the moment God made His children He stopped, ceased and stilled everything with a Sabbath day to make sure we stayed connected to Him. (Genesis 2:2,3)

See how Jesus gets angry (Mark 3) and even indignant (Luke 13) when some misuse the Sabbath obscuring joy and freedom God longed for people to experience. Jesus argues (Matthew 12:1-8) and urges (Luke 14:1-6) people to pay attention to the central purpose of Sabbath. The Sabbath is not lost when Jesus heals on the Sabbath as a window to God's heart (John 9) and punctuates how short-sighted and blind we become when people forget to remember the reason for our existence. (John 5:1-18, John 7:17-24)

Look at the new believers in the Christian church (Jews and Gentiles) meeting from Sabbath to Sabbath as though it were the most normal thing in the world to do. (Acts 13:13-15; 16:12-14;15:21;17:1-3; 18:3-5) Furthermore, examine the way the writer of Hebrews deepens the meaning of Sabbath rest by connecting it to our journey as believers who are pressing toward the Promised Land. (Hebrews 4:1-11) From the beginning of the Bible to the end God reminds us to stay connected to Him as Creator and Savior. (Revelation 4:6-11, Revelation 14:7)

Storytelling

The second half of this week focuses on the exercise of storytelling—telling our story of God's power and grace. Stories make memories vivid and enduring, but they also stitch together what is meaningful in the tapestry of our lives. Stories are the most effective teaching tool as well as the most memorable.

Ivan Illich, an Austrian philosopher and anarchist, was asked how one could make the greatest change on society. He replied: "Neither revolution nor reformation can ultimately change a society. Rather, you must tell a powerful tale, one so persuasive that it sweeps away the old myths and becomes a preferred story. If you want to change society, then you have to tell an alternative story."[1]

Eugene Peterson observed: "We live in a world impoverished of story. Words in our culture are a form of currency used mostly to provide information. Contemporary schooling is primarily an exercise in piling up information. By the time we have completed our assigned years in the classroom, we have far more information than we will ever be able to put to use."[2]

Before the pen or keyboard, there was the story and the memory. The stories in Genesis are only known today because people committed the events to memory and systematically told them so they might endure.

Storytelling paints a wide-angled picture of the meaning of our purpose on earth. There is no other real story, other than the great narrative of God and people. Nothing colors the canvas of our lives like stories that reveal the big picture. And no event stands out on the mural of human life as Calvary. At the cross we see who God is and who we are. We see how we are bound to God. We see the event of the resurrection and witness first-hand that God is working His plan to bring us home. What a story!

Storytelling enables us to remember, and our remembering gives birth to hope. Hope is the theme of our story. Our task is to learn how we enter into and relate to the one true story of God and people.

DAY 29 · IS THAT A TRICK QUESTION?

"Another time Jesus went into the synagogue, and a man with a shriveled hand was there. Some of them were looking for a reason to accuse Jesus, so they watched him closely to see if he would heal him on the Sabbath. Jesus said to the man with the shriveled hand, "Stand up in front of everyone." Then Jesus asked them, "Which is lawful on the Sabbath: to do good or to do evil, to save life or to kill?" But they remained silent. He looked around at them in anger and, deeply distressed at their stubborn hearts, said to the man, "Stretch out your hand." He stretched it out, and his hand was completely restored. Then the Pharisees went out and began to plot with the Herodians how they might kill Jesus." (Mark 3:1-6)

I often wonder if some questions are meant to convey a truth rather than invite an answer. Here are a few I can recall from my own experience:

When I took apart the vacuum cleaner my parents looked at me in wonder and asked, "What were you thinking?" I was petty sure they did not want to know the answer to that question.

One evening my mother carried all the groceries in by herself, but when she lifted the groceries to put them on the table the bags tore and all the contents spilled out on the floor. In frustration she just looked at me and said, "Are you just going to stand there or are you going to help?" I wanted to answer, "If I was too lazy to help you with the groceries when they were all nicely packaged in bags, what makes you think I would want to help when they are laying all unorganized on the floor?"

Returning home from an all day event my wife came home to a kitchen that was decimated by my attempts to cook various unique and untried recipes. Scanning the kitchen she could barely recognize the place. She inquired, "Do you have any idea what a mess you made?" I did—a big one. But I felt like that wasn't the answer she was looking for.

Some questions Jesus asked are more thought provoking while other inquiries call for action. Some questions prompt self-examination and others invite you to believe something new about God. Consider some of the questions Jesus asked:

If the salt loses its saltiness, how will it become salty again?

If you love those who love you, what reward do you have? Don't the tax collectors do the same?

Why are you worried about clothing?

Which is easier to say, "'Your sins are forgiven,' or 'get up and walk'?"

Why are you afraid?

Do you believe that I am able to do this?

Who is greater, the one who reclines at the table or the one who serves?

Who do you think I am?

What is written in the Law—how does it read to you?

Which of these three proved to be the neighbor?

What do you want me to do for you?

Do you love me?

The Pharisees accused Jesus of breaking the Sabbath by healing a man with a withered hand, which prompted Jesus to ask, "Which is lawful on the Sabbath: to do good or to do evil, to save life or to kill?" If you actually answer the question you are going to look foolish because the right answer is so unmistakably obvious (The answer is "doing good" and "saving life"—Just in case). To not answer demonstrates you were wrong to push the issue in the first place. Either way, He has got you. And hopefully, you got the point.

It is simple: Do good, save life. If your framework for the Sabbath begins with these two endeavors you will know what God was thinking when he called you to enter in Sabbath rest.

The Pharisees and the Scribes were not always such a pain in the neck. Originally, they were the ones who tried to keep the Hebrew faith true during seasons of moral, ethical, and intellectual bankruptcy. The Pharisees and Scribes truly were the most passionate people of faith and duty to God. And in order to preserve the rich beauty of God's law and the history of God's people, they made rules and subsets and tried to capture every scenario that might trip a believer up in their walk with God. Over time, this devotion deformed into an endless catalogue of unbelievably tedious rules regarding Sabbath keeping.

William Barclay comments:

"One of the things which are forbidden is the carrying of a burden. Immediately the scribe asks: 'What is a burden?' So in the Mishnah there is definition after definition of what constitutes a burden—milk enough for a gulp, honey enough to put on a sore, oil enough to anoint the smallest member, water enough to rub off an eye-plaster, leather enough to make an amulet, ink enough to write two letters of the alphabet, coarse sand enough to cover a plasterer's trowel, reed enough to make a pen, a pebble big enough to throw at a bird, anything which weighs as much as two dried figs."[3]

These rules were set up so people could obey and wouldn't even have to think about it. The *last thing* God wanted was for us *not* to think about it. The last thing God wanted for us was not to think about *Him*, which is why Jesus throws down a rhetorical—logical question, "Which is lawful on the Sabbath: to do good or to do evil, to save life or to kill?"

What might happen if we were to answer Jesus' question with action and simply frame our next Sabbath by the virtues of "doing good" and "saving life?" Surely the Sabbath would become more than a list of scheduled events or an endless nap. What would your Sabbath look like?

Make a list of activities that are eminently doable along the lines of "doing good" and "saving life." Start making a plan today to prepare for these kinds of experiences on your next Sabbath day. Invite a few friends to join you in the activity.

Reflect on the following question: If you were to live each Sabbath day based on the notion of doing good and saving life, do you think your day would be more or less restful?

DAY 30 · ABRAHAM'S ORPHAN

"On a Sabbath Jesus was teaching in one of the synagogues, and a woman was there who had been crippled by a spirit for eighteen years. She was bent over and could not straighten up at all. When Jesus saw her, he called her forward and said to her, "Woman, you are set free from your infirmity." Then he put his hands on her, and immediately she straightened up and praised God. Indignant because Jesus had healed on the Sabbath, the synagogue leader said to the people, "There are six days for work. So come and be healed on those days, not on the Sabbath." The Lord answered him, "You hypocrites! Doesn't each of you on the Sabbath untie your ox or donkey from the stall and lead it out to give it water? Then should not this woman, a daughter of Abraham, whom Satan has kept bound for eighteen long years, be set free on the Sabbath day from what bound her?" When he said this, all his opponents were humiliated, but the people were delighted with all the wonderful things he was doing."(Luke 13:10-17)

She had been crippled, bent over and broken by this illness for eighteen years. She knew every cobblestone and was intimately familiar with every pothole in town because that is all she saw. Her eyes were always in the gutters and grime of the streets and never in the tops of the trees or birds flying against the backdrop of the clear blue sky. 936 times she made her way on the Sabbath day and 936 times she came back disappointed, bent over, and empty. On the 937 Sabbath, everything changed.

Luke tells the story of how "when Jesus saw her" He uncorked like a bottle of sparkling cider, popping with unchecked disapproval at the inhumane treatment of a woman who had been crippled for eighteen years. The religious leaders did not physically attack her, but they committed what can be an even more severe act of disdain, they dismissed her. They overlooked her. Her name. Her value. Her condition. Her identity.

Had she given up? Perhaps she was sick and tired of being sick and tired. And according to Jesus, nothing is more appropriate to do on the Sabbath day than helping someone find rest. Likewise, there is nothing more offensive than getting in the way of those who are broken and enslaved by life when they are hoping to be set free.

First of all, Jesus calls her forward, stands her up and heals her. Secondly, Jesus called the president of the synagogue a "hypocrite" because they would not celebrate when a daughter of Abraham had been healed. They treated their animals with greater devotion than this lady. It was part of the tradition of the Jews to treat beasts of burden with kindness, hence, setting the animal free and leading it to water was well within the boundaries of Sabbath-keeping. Being nice to animals is not hypocritical. Being nice to animals and mean to people is fakery. To be aware of the needs of a donkey and indifferent to the pain of a child of God is sin. Thirdly, Jesus notices the woman and reminds everyone that she is in fact a daughter of Abraham.

This woman found rest as well as freedom that came from knowing that she is a destined daughter of God. Her story reminds me of Melba Beals.

Melba Beals was one of nine black teenage girls who were chosen to integrate Central High in 1957. In the book Warriors Don't Cry, she begins by telling the story that has become what I would call a Sabbath for her. An event that stood as a constant reminder of who she was and what made her truly significant.

When she was born the doctor had to use forceps, which injured her scalp, which resulted in a serious infection a few days later. Melba's mom took her to the white hospital that reluctantly took care of the families of the black men who worked on the railroad. In order to save her life the doctor surgically placed a drainage system beneath her scalp but her condition did not get better. Her mom tried to get the doctors and nurses to examine the baby girl but they would not taker her seriously brushing her off saying, "Just give it time." After a couple of days her temperature hit 106 and the little baby began to convulse, and so the family called the minister and family to gather for last rites.

At the hospital her grandmother was rocking her back and forth singing to her while her mother paced nervously around the room. A black janitor sweeping in the hallway inquired her mother was crying and she explained that little Melba was dying because they couldn't stop the infection in her head. The old janitor extended his sadness and commented something about how the Epsom salts hadn't worked as prescribed. Melba's mother ran after him and asked him what he meant by "Epsom salts."

Melba tells the story:

"He explained that a couple of days before he had been cleaning the operating room as they had finished up with the surgery. He heard the doctor tell the white nurse to irrigate my head with Epsom salts and warm water every two or three hours or I wouldn't make it.

Mother shouted the words "Epsom salts and water" as she raced down the hall desperately searching for a nurse. The woman was indignant, saying, yes, come to think of it, the doctor had said something about Epsom salts. "But we don't coddle your kind," she growled.

Mother didn't talk back to the nurse. Instead, she sent for Epsom salts and began the treatment right away. Within two days, I was remarkably better. The minister went home, and the sisters from the church abandoned their death-watch, declaring they had witnessed a miracle."[4]

Melba Beals was selected to integrate Central High she remembered how God spared her life and had chosen her to carry the banner for her people. Knowing who she was anchor for what she would become.

Perhaps today you need a reminder of who God is and who you are in Christ. The question Christ asked the people that day He asks on your behalf today, "Doesn't this child of Abraham deserve the freedom that comes from real, Sabbath rest?"

What does it look like to set someone free in your world today? What are the ways in which people feel trapped? As you start the day, consider thoughtfully the people you expect to meet and the ways in which you can liberate them from something that chains them. Some are chained by low expectations. Others are chained by greed. Some might feel free if they could just be counted as valuable.

Reflect on those you expect to meet and those who you may meet unexpectedly. Pray and watch for the opportunities to practice the art of Sabbath today.

DAY 31 · CUSTOM EYES YOUR LIFE

"Jesus returned to Galilee in the power of the Spirit, and news about him spread through the whole countryside. He was teaching in their synagogues, and everyone praised him. He went to Nazareth, where he had been brought up, and on the Sabbath day he went into the synagogue, as was his custom. He stood up to read, and the scroll of the prophet Isaiah was handed to him. Unrolling it, he found the place where it is written:

"The Spirit of the Lord is on me,
because he has anointed me
to proclaim good news to the poor.
He has sent me to proclaim freedom for the prisoners
and recovery of sight for the blind,
to set the oppressed free,
to proclaim the year of the Lord's favor."

Then he rolled up the scroll, gave it back to the attendant and sat down. The eyes of everyone in the synagogue were fastened on him. He began by saying to them, "Today this scripture is fulfilled in your hearing." (Luke 4:14-21)

Everything we think and do is shaped or informed by assumptions we hold but may not even be aware—a worldview. Another way to describe how humans have "custom eyes" is that we see life through our own unique set of lenses. Knowing *about* the lens we see life through is an important part of maturity.

In the reading today we see that even Jesus looks at the world through a particular lens. The Son of God comes to the synagogue, as it is *His practice*, and reads from Isaiah 61 what might be His personal vision statement. This particular passage "handed to Him" was a Sabbath favorite because it demonstrates the promise of God's glory to Israel and later in the passage—vengeance on the gentiles. The gentiles were considered to "fuel for the fires of hell" by Jews, which brings us to the moment that the people turned on their "fair haired boy from Nazareth." What did Jesus do to set them off?

He stopped reading. He didn't finish. He ended His reading without going into the "vengeance" part destined for the outsiders. When they pressed Jesus on this issue He names two gentiles in the Old Testament: Naaman (who conquered Israel and sent them to Babylon by God's power—ouch!), and the Shunamite widow who experienced the miraculous blessing of provision in the worst of times.

Let's just say that the worldview of Jesus and that of the Jews clashed in this moment like two cars headed toward each other on a one-way street. The good news Jesus came to proclaim was for the "whole world," for everyone! Check out what the prophet Isaiah reported from God a few chapters before:

"Suppose **outsiders** want to follow me

and serve me.

They want to **love me**

and **worship me**.

They keep the Sabbath day and do not misuse it.

And they are **faithful** in keeping **my covenant**.

Then I will bring them to my holy mountain of Zion.

I will give them joy in my house.

They can **pray** there.

I will **accept their burnt offerings and sacrifices on my altar**.

My house will be called

a house where people from **all nations** can pray."

The Lord and King will gather

those who were taken away from their homes in Israel.

He announces, "I will gather them to myself.

And **I will gather others to join them**." (Isaiah 56:1-8)

I highlighted and underlined the above portions to underscore how God viewed the world and how the Jews custom-eyes their practice of faith in God. What a shift in thinking! Can you imagine how the Jews would have been punched in the gut by such news, especially if it were considered to be "good news."

There are two beautiful qualities that emerge from the Person of Christ on this Sabbath day. The *custom* of Sabbath's original purpose and the *cause* that God's people were supposed to take up as an outgrowth of their practice.

THE CUSTOM

The word "custom" has the connotation of "practice" or "habit." The significance rang like a bell in my mind: People who know *how to stop* know *how to see*. These are the ones that observe the broken world around us and give their time, money, and personal space to make a difference. These are a collective of both visionaries and doers. For some, the doing awakens the vision. For others, they stop and see and therefore know what to do.

When you make stopping (Sabbath) a practice you will consequently see the needs of others around you. But keep in mind, if you don't practice your "vision statement" or what "you see" because of your Sabbath, you may lose your way. People who stop and see *can* help the broken, the outsiders, and the forgotten— but they don't always do it.

THE CAUSE

If you don't actively practice "proclaiming good news to the poor" and "freedom for the prisoners" and "recovery of sight for the blind" and "set the oppressed free" and "proclaiming the year of the Lord's favor," then you will be one of those blind people who think you see just fine.

Engage today in God's old way of stopping and seeing—then do it. What might your next Sabbath be like if you were to do what you see in Jesus' example?

 What are some of the assumptions you have about life, Sabbath, and service to outsiders? Reflect on some of your experiences that you think have shaped your "worldview."

Good news to the poor

Freedom from the prisoners

Sight for the blind

What can you do today to practice one or all three of these goals? Again, you have to take to think about what the "poor, blind and imprisoned" look like in your world—your sphere of influence. There are probably more than we can imagine.

DAY 32 · THE GIFT IS FOR YOU

"One Sabbath Jesus was going through the grainfields, and as his disciples walked along, they began to pick some heads of grain. The Pharisees said to him, "Look, why are they doing what is unlawful on the Sabbath?" He answered, "Have you never read what David did when he and his companions were hungry and in need? In the days of Abiathar the high priest, he entered the house of God and ate the consecrated bread, which is lawful only for priests to eat. And he also gave some to his companions." Then he said to them, "The Sabbath was made for man, not man for the Sabbath. So the Son of Man is Lord even of the Sabbath." (Mark 2:23-27)

We need rest—not rules. Did you know?

In Oklahoma, you can be arrested for making ugly faces at a dog.

In Salt Lake County, Utah, it's illegal to walk down the street carrying a violin in a paper bag.

In San Francisco, it's illegal to pile horse manure more than six feet high on a street corner.

In California it is illegal for a vehicle without a driver to exceed 60 miles per hour.

In Tennessee, you are breaking the law if you drive while sleeping.

In New York, the penalty for jumping off a building is: Death.

In Danville, Pennsylvania, all fire hydrants must be checked one hour before all fires.

In Pennsylvania, it's against the law to tie a dollar bill on a string on the ground and pull it away when someone tries to pick it up.

In France, it is against the law to sell dolls that do not have human faces.

The Pharisees and Teachers of the law asked, "Why are they doing what is unlawful on the Sabbath?"

Clearly, the institution of the Sabbath had become bigger than the people who were supposed to experience rest. Later in Mark 2:28 Jesus replied, "The Sabbath was made for man, not man for the Sabbath."

When they religious leaders sought to trap Jesus in Jerusalem the Lord them by saying to the people gathered:

"Instead of giving you God's Law as food and drink by which you can banquet on God, they package it in bundles of rules, loading you down like pack animals. They seem to take pleasure in watching you stagger under these loads, and wouldn't think of lifting a finger to help." (Matthew 23:4,5, *The Message*)

Perhaps you feel like a pack animal, carrying a burden day after day. Or maybe you feel a little like Tattoo—the basset hound.

A Tacoma, Washington, newspaper carried the story of Tattoo. The dog didn't intend to go for an evening run, but when his owner shut his leash in the car door and took off for a drive with Tattoo still outside the vehicle, he had no choice.

Motorcycle officer Terry Filbert noticed a passing vehicle with something following behind it: it was "the basset hound picking [up his feet] and putting them down as fast as he could." He chased the car to a stop. Tattoo was rescued, but not before the dog had reached a speed of 20 to 25 miles per hour.

Too many of us end up living like Tattoo, our days marked by picking up our paws putting them down as fast as we can. There is no vision. No thinking. No sharing. No time to listen or be a friend. No way to learn something new. No way to give of yourself or receive a gift graciously. Too many don't even know how to rest and be awake at the same time.

One Friday evening a handful of college students were lounging around my house after a meal when I noticed Janelle starting to nod off. Afraid she would sprain her eyelids jerking them open forcing herself to stay awake I asked, "Why don't just go home and go to sleep?" She slurred a well-thought-out response: "No. I want to just stay here for a little while. I'm never resting and awake at the same time." In some cases sleep only postpones our exhaustion for a few more hours, but as soon as the day begins, the children argue, the bills arrive, hospital calls—our sense of purpose and our quest for freedom get squeezed out by a deep hunger for rest.

Recent survey reports that:

67% of people feel they need a long vacation

66% of people often feel stressed

60% of people feel time is crunched

51% of people want less work

49% of people feel pressured to succeed

48% of feel overwhelmed

Studies also show that many first time marathon runners return to training too soon without getting proper rest. John Henderson, a columnist for *Runner's World*, says, "Runners make the incorrect assumption that once the soreness in muscles is gone, then they are recovered. But thousands of microscopic tears in the muscles can take four to six weeks for complete healing."[5]

From every angle of life we see evidence that we are meant to work hard, but also rest well. We can be busy, yet we are able to just "be." When the religious leaders freak out over grabbing some grain by the wayside you have to wonder if they too had no idea of what it means to "enter into rest." The writer of Hebrews urges believers to experientially "enter in" what God offers us as a gift.

"Therefore, since the promise of entering his rest still stands, let us be careful that none of you be found to have fallen short of it...There remains, then, a

Sabbath-rest for the people of God; for anyone who enters God's rest also rests from his own work, just as God did from his. Let us, therefore, make every effort to enter that rest, so that no one will fall by following their example of disobedience." (Hebrews 4:1-11)

Step into the rest!

Enter in: Choose a door or a gate you have access to but rarely use to practice the experience of "entering in." Perhaps you might go into a store or building but before you go through the door, think about what you want to be different about your next Sabbath. Reflect. Plan. Pray. Remember, you have entered a different place your normal everyday traffic will take you to. Reflect on how "entering into the Sabbath" can be like going into a different place. What do you see, smell, hear and feel as you abide there?

DAY 33 · HER STORY WILL BE TOLD

While he was in Bethany, reclining at the table in the home of a man known as Simon the Leper, a woman came with an alabaster jar of very expensive perfume, made of pure nard. She broke the jar and poured the perfume on his head. Some of those present were saying indignantly to one another, "Why this waste of perfume? It could have been sold for more than a year's wages and the money given to the poor." And they rebuked her harshly. "Leave her alone," said Jesus. "Why are you bothering her? She has done a beautiful thing to me. The poor you will always have with you, and you can help them any time you want. But you will not always have me. She did what she could. She poured perfume on my body beforehand to prepare for my burial. I tell you the truth, wherever the gospel is preached throughout the world, what she has done will also be told, in memory of her." (Mark 14:3-9)

Defining moments often come when we least expect them. Consider the way one decision transformed a pilot's perspective on life:

On a commuter flight from Portland, Maine, to Boston, pilot Henry Dempsey heard an unusual noise at the rear of the small aircraft. He turned the controls over to his copilot and went back to check it out. As he reached the tail section, the plane hit some turbulence, and Dempsey was tossed against the rear door. He quickly discovered the source of the mysterious noise. The rear door had not been latched properly, and it flew open. He was instantly sucked out of the jet.

The copilot immediately radioed the nearest airport, requesting permission to make an emergency landing. He reported the loss of the pilot, and asked that a helicopter search the area of the ocean they had been flying over.[6]

A defining moment. One choice. A quick decision. An idea you just had to try. You leap and learn. There comes a moment in your life where you have to leap into the unknown and embrace what lies ahead. In the movie Tin Cup, Kevin Costner plays a maverick golfer with the tendency to spout poetry or philosophy as the moment dictates. One of his famous lines is: "When a defining moment comes, you either define the moment or the moment defines you." Both can be said of the woman who anointed Jesus. The woman who came to Christ purchased the box of perfume, equaling a "year's wages." It doesn't matter what the exchange rate is, it was "a year's wages." Do the math for yourself; This is a woman who had to live differently because of the gift she gave.

How much faith does it take to walk into a room and give a gift? Read the story again and imagine what she endured to complete this task. Compare the sneers and whispers, the names and the scorn, with the adoration she received and the joy of her service in Mark 14:9:

"I tell you the truth, wherever the gospel is preached throughout the world, what she has done will also be told, in memory of her."

There are special acts of grace we might do for others, but to embrace public humiliation, even retaliation for the chance to bring a blessing to Jesus is truly a beautiful act of faith. The woman's gift became the earmark for the gospel! I don't think for a moment she was trying to get into the hall of fame of faith. But her gift was received and her voice was heard. Now, her story will continue to be told throughout the ages.

What seems so amazing is that defining moments don't often present themselves as pivotal events. A defining moment usually disguises itself in the ordinary events of the day. A co-worker takes a little more time to listen to a hurting person and a floodgate opens and a new relationship begins. A student volunteers a little bit of time and catches the bug of service, which causes him to re-orient his entire career. Ordinary things. Jesus said, "She did what she could." The defining moments come in ordinary packages, but the results of action are extraordinary things.

The rest of the story turns out like this:

After the plane landed, they found Henry Dempsey—holding onto the outdoor ladder of the aircraft. Somehow he had caught the ladder, held on for ten minutes as the plane flew 200 mph at an altitude of 4,000 feet, and then, upon landing, kept his head from hitting the runway, which was a mere twelve inches away. It took airport personnel several minutes to pry Dempsey's fingers from the ladder.[7]

Do you think Henry will ever see life the same way again? Hopefully, when you practice telling your story of faith, the door you open will not be as dramatic. You never know for sure, you just step out as though you are certain.

 Do you have a moment ahead that could be a defining moment? Maybe there is a decision you need to make or a deliberate attempt to talk to someone about Christ. Talk to God openly in prayer about the specific step you feel you need to take. Reflect on some of the Biblical examples of faith in Hebrews 11. Try to imagine some of the leaps the ancient heroes of faith had to take. Who do you identify with most and why?

DAY 34 · BEFORE AND AFTER PICTURES

"They went across the lake to the region of the Gerasenes. When Jesus got out of the boat, a man with an impure spirit came from the tombs to meet him. This man lived in the tombs, and no one could bind him anymore, not even with a chain. For he had often been chained hand and foot, but he tore the chains apart and broke the irons on his feet. No one was strong enough to subdue him. Night and day among the tombs and in the hills he would cry out and cut himself with stones...As Jesus was getting into the boat, the man who had been demon-possessed begged to go with him. Jesus did not let him, but said, "Go home to your own people and tell them how much the Lord has done for you, and how he has had mercy on you." So the man went away and began to tell in the Decapolis how much Jesus had done for him. And all the people were amazed."(Mark 5:1-5, 18-20)

Recently, my curiosity has caused me to meander into a strange, even dangerous, part of society: Tabloid/magazine stands at the checkout area. It's embarrassing, but I have been scanning and searching all the "before and after" pictures that compel people to do or buy something to augment their appearance. It's research. I had no hypothesis—only a notion that there might be some method to the "before and after" phenomenon.

Two insights emerged in my observations of before and after pictures: 1) So many people are aching to change. The temptation to transform skin, hair, weight, muscles, wrinkles, spots, color, clothes, and image is overwhelming, and 2) The "after" pictures usually show the person genuinely smiling, eyes are open wide, better lighting, and ultimately, they just appear happier. There is a deliberate attempt to portray the idea that if the outside is different, you will be a different person on the inside.

BEFORE AND AFTER

In the reading for today we encounter a young man who is transformed by his encounter with Jesus, and the change is so real that you might not even recognize him.

Imagine what the demoniac's before and after pictures might look like. Read Mark 4 and 5 to consider the setting of the story. Prior to the encounter with the demoniac, Jesus and the disciples cross the lake when a furious storm brings them to a near death experience—the nerves of the disciples were already frayed. The whole mood of this event is eerie. This story takes place late the same evening of the storm. It is dark by the lakeside. A scream comes from the woods in the distance. The sound of terror and agony, mixed with uncontrollable rage makes its way closer and closer. Then, a man violently breaks through the bushes on the edge of the beach and runs towards you. In any time or place, the oncoming demoniac would strike fear in anyone.

Read what life was like for the one who was a slave of "legion," a whole platoon of demons. (verses 1-5) I used to wonder if the demons were real or some psychological disorder, but Jesus speaks to a real being and it answers. It was real.

If you have ever had a moment where you came close to death then you know how that fear can grip you—even change you. Even though the man possessed rages with profanities, Jesus saw a spot of his poor heart untouched by evil—a desperate cry for mercy. What a scene. What a Savior—He knows us at our worst and somehow He can see the sleeping hero inside. The disciples flee but Christ steps forward and commands the demons to flee. It was real!

When the town folk heard what happened they came and "saw the man who had been possessed by the legion of demons, sitting there, **dressed and in his right mind**; and they were afraid." A couple of questions remain.

Why does Jesus allow the demons to go to the pigs? Could it be that the boy needed to see the demons going into something else? Tangible. Real. Unmistakable evidence that he was free. Throughout the day he might be okay, but one would almost naturally fear the awful demons returning in the dark of the night. Maybe seeing the demons enter something else actualized his freedom.

Why was the man so desperate to go in the boat with Jesus? Perhaps he is clinging to Jesus, calling "shotgun" and grabbing the front seat in the boat for the same reason he needed to see the demons enter the pigs. He doesn't want them to come back. The freedom is real, but so were the demons. The change is real, but will it last?

Compassionate but firm, Jesus gives this poster boy for "before and after" pictures a prescription to keep the demons away: "Go home to your own people and tell them how much the Lord has done for you, and how he has had mercy on you."

There is a liberation that comes from saying what God has done for you. The very expression, written or spoken, will etch the experience deeper in your heart. Telling the simple story of "what God has done for you and how He has had mercy on you" is a non-negotiable exercise of those who would follow Christ. Could this boy return to his home and *not* say anything. Could he just be an example? No, they would ask.

Can you hear him share his story? "Let me tell you what Jesus did for me..." Before there was Peter and John, there was an unnamed man who peppered the region that the apostles would one day go to with the story of Jesus. Later, the apostles would echo the words of the demoniac in their own stories. Read them in the Into the Wild section and begin to write your own story of "what God has done for you, and how He has had mercy on you."

Take a few moments throughout the day to stop and read the different storied testimonies of those who knew Christ. At the end of the day begin to write your story—your testimony that simply follows the outline Christ gave the demoniac: What has God done for you? How has He had mercy on you? Tuck the written page in your Bible and be ready to share it with someone if the opportunity should arise.

Paul (Acts 9 and 26)   Peter (2 Peter 1:16)   John (1 John 1:1-4)

DAY 35 · SHE SAID HE SAID

"Many of the Samaritans from that town believed in him because of the woman's testimony, "He told me everything I ever did." So, when the Samaritans came to him, they urged him to stay with them, and he stayed two days. And because of his words many more became believers. They said to the woman, "We no longer believe just because of what you said; now we have heard for ourselves, and we know that this man really is the Savior of the world." (John 4:39-42)

In the introduction for this week the idea of storytelling is offered as an exercise—a practice that will give God access to a part of our lives in a new and meaningful way. We tell stories all the time.

Annette Simons in *The Story Factor*, shares the story that set her on a quest to understand how stories shape our life:

"In 1992, I sat in the cool October breeze, surrounded by 400 others in a tent in Jonesborough, Tennessee, waiting to hear the next storyteller. The group ranged from rich to poor, city types to country folk, professors to sixth-grade graduates. Next to me was a gray-bearded farmer-type in overalls with an "NRA" button on his cap. As an African American man got up to speak, this man turned to his wife and whispered something in an irritated tone...he folded his arms and started examining the construction of the tent's roof. The African American storyteller began to tell us of his story of a lonely night during the 1960s deep in the heart of Mississippi. He and six other activists feared the dangers they would face by marching the next morning. He described how they stared into the campfire, as one of them began to sing. The singing calmed their fears. His story was so real we could feel the fear and see the light of the campfire. Then he asked us to sing with him. We did. "Swing Low, Sweet Chariot" vibrated out of our throats like a big 400-pie organ. Next to me, the farmer sang too. I saw a tear roll down his rough red cheek. I had just witnessed the power of a story."[8]

Simmons describes the ripple effect of storytelling and makes a strong case for re-organizing our approach to business, society, religion, and life in general—through storytelling.

The Samaritan woman's encounter has been told in countless sermons, but the impact of her conversation with Christ started a fire in Samaria that none of the disciples could start. Clearly, the prejudice between Jew and Gentile had so divided the two cultures that occupied the same region, that any attempts to share "the gospel" were rejected.

Notice, again the simplicity of the woman's story: "I met a man who told me everything I ever did." It wasn't really totally accurate. It lacked all the technical features of a story. There is no clever introductions or a gripping climax. But the fire spread. The people of Samaria listened, and came to Jesus to witness the fire that caused this woman to come alive—firsthand.

We so desperately need believers today to meet this same Jesus, and tell their story of His grace to the next generation. We need new storytellers who keep the flame of God's power burning bright in a world that is changing.

"In the early days of the Tennessee Valley Project, a dilapidated log homestead had to be abandoned to make room for a lake behind the dam. A new home on the hillside had already been erected for the cabin's poor Appalachian family, but they refused to move into their beautiful new split-level ranch ("splanch," as they called it).

The day of the flooding arrived, but still the family refused to move. As the bulldozers were brought in, the Appalachian family brought out their shotguns. No amount of legal brandishing or bulldozer menacing would budge this family from their cabin. Then someone from the TVA decided to try one last-ditch effort to end the stalemate. They called in a social worker to talk with the family and find out what their problem was.

"We ain't goin' anywhere," the family announced to the social worker. "Nobody can make us. We're not budging no matter how many threats you make or how rundown our li'l cabin may look to you!"

The social worker pleaded, "Help me to explain to the authorities why you won't move into your beautiful new home."

"See that fire over there?" the man asked, pointing to a blazing fire in the primitive hearth of the log cottage. "My grandpa built that fire over a hundred years ago," the man explained. "He never let it go out, for he had no matches and it was a long way to a neighbor's. Then my pa tended the fire, and since he died, I've tended it. None of us ever let it die, and I ain't a-goin' to move away now and let grandpa's fire go out!"

This gave the social worker an idea. She arranged for a large apple butter kettle to be delivered to the home. She explained to the family that they could scoop up the live coals from the fire and carry them to the new home where they would then be poured out and fresh kindling added. In this way grandpa's fire need never go out. Would this be acceptable? This Appalachian family huddled, and then agreed to move from their shack in the hollow up to the new home on the hillside.

All of their belongings were moved but they never let the kettle with the burning coals out of their sight. The family wouldn't budge until they could take with them the fire of their ancestors."[9]

Many have risked their lives to be a part of this story. Will you enter in, tell your story, and carry the flame forward?

Write yourself into His Story. Make a historical timeline with all the events you can remember off the top of your head. (If you look in your Bible you may find a sample among the maps) Include the storied lives of key people whose contribution to humanity is unforgettable. Enter in yourself with a mark in the same way you have included others. You are part of the story of God and people.

1   Tony and Felicity Dale, George Barna, The Rabbit and the Elephant: (Tyndale, 2009) p. 133.

2   Eugene Peterson, Introduction to the Stories of Jesus: (NavPress, 1999) p. 1.

3   William Barclay, The Mind of Christ, 152,153.

4   Melba Beals, Warriors Don't Cry, (Washington Square Press, New York, NY, 1994) p.5.

5   Bob Condor, *At Ease*: Chicago Tribune, October 23 1997, sec. 5 p. 6.

6   Dan Schaeffer, Defining Moments, (Grand Rapids, Michigan: Discovery House, 2000) p. 113, 114.

7   Ibid, p. 113, 114.

8   Annette Simmons, The Story Factor: (Basic Books, New York, 2002) p.

9   Troy Fitzgerald, Live Like You Mean It, (Pacific Press Publishing Association: Nampa, ID, 2010) p. 182,183.

Small Group Questions—
SABBATH AND STORYTELLING

What story in the life of Christ spoke to you this week? Why?

How is the exercise of keeping Sabbath both a "discipline" and a "blessing?"

What areas of your life do you need to stop, cease, and still on a regular basis?
How does Sabbath relate to your hectic life?

There is now a more common conversation going on the world about Sabbath.
Not as much as "when" the Sabbath is as to how much people need to rest. In what
way is "the Sabbath" more relevant today than ever?

What activities and experiences do you think do the most good, save the most lives,
and offer the most rest on a Sabbath day?

How do you think technology has enhanced the possibilities of "telling the story
of God and people" and how might it be hindering people form hearing the great
narrative today?

In John 19:35, 20:31, 21:24,25 John refers to the stories He wrote about Jesus
and the stories he left out. How do these verses affect the way you read the stories
in the Bible?

If you had to share 3-5 stories from your life that shape "who you are" today,
which stories would you tell?

Have you written out your story—your testimony? Sometimes it is easier to make
headings that are topical or thematic, and then ask: What stories would I tell from
my experience about these topics. Another way to start practicing your storytelling
is to think of the questions people ask about the meaning of life, faith and the
challenges we face day to day. List the questions and think/write out stories form
your experience that you would use to respond to those questions.

—WEEK 6—
Fasting (and Feasting)

As we enter into the final week of *Forty Days Wild* it seems appropriate to conclude this journey with a season of fasting and feasting. In a way the two exercises are related, but not as polar opposites. When we refer to fasting it is the laying aside or deliberate bending of your appetite so that you might more keenly respond to God's leading in your life. Likewise, feasting is surprisingly difficult for some because you are called upon to celebrate—even when you don't feel like it. Both are battles where you win when you surrender.

Fasting

A traditional definition of fasting is, "Going without food or drink voluntarily, generally for religious purposes." The definition sounds a bit sterile, but it is more or less accurate. But what good is it? Fasting, as Arthur Wallis says in his book *God's Chosen Fast*, is a way of teaching our bodies to be our servants rather than our masters! What fasting may do, that nothing else can, is get us used to depending on God completely—for everything.

Here are a few thoughts about fasting:

Dallas Willard claims, "Fasting must forever center on God. It must be God-initiated and God-ordained...Fasting confirms our utter dependence upon God by finding in him a source of sustenance beyond food."[1]

"In fasting we learn to suffer happily as we feast on God. And it is a good lesson, because in our lives we will suffer, no matter what else happens to us... This discipline teaches us a lot about ourselves very quickly."[2]

The Apostle Paul explains:

"Athletes exercise self-control in all things... So I do not run aimlessly... but I punish my body and enslave it, so that after proclaiming to others I myself should not be disqualified." (1 Corinthians 9:25-27)

While Paul sounds a bit like a sadist, he is perhaps one of the most brutally honest with the whole tension between the heart and the spirit—the flesh and the will. Paul confesses, "For I have the desire to do what is good, but I cannot carry it out. For I do not do the good I want to do, but the evil I do not want to do—this I keep on doing... (Romans 7:18,19)

Fasting is a way to exercise the will that works in you. In a discussion with several students about the "the time of the end," one student admitted, "When it is a life or death decision—I know I will not cave in. I'll stand up for God."

I thought about how bold that statement was, and how many of us have probably thought the same at one point or another. The conversation was about our loyalty to God in the hard times as opposed to the easy times. It is a misguided notion to think that what you can't seem to do now (when it seems easy) will be easier to do when it's harder (under serious persecution). The truth is that if you can't be honest with a dollar, you're not going to have integrity with a thousand. If you can't love your family—how will you be loving to those people you don't know or like?

Fasting builds the ability to master your will. Fasting is not for show, but an exercise that enables you to grow. You grow in confidence that you don't always have to have what you want when you want it. You grow in your ability to choose wisely when your emotions cry out for foolishness. You grow in your ability to be courageous, not because you might feel good, but because it is right.

Consider fasting as way to work out a muscle that may be weak in your life. Actually, being "strong willed" is not always a character flaw. It can be taken to excess, but strong willed people tend to be able to kick addictions, make tough choices, save money, you name it!

Give fasting a try with your time, entertainment, food, relationships, or even your hobbies.

Feasting

God is the greatest giver, biggest partier, and a scandalous banquet thrower. He is accused of bringing out the best drink when everyone expects less. He is famous for making meals with baskets and baskets of leftovers. God is the one who will eat and drink with sinners and knows how to sit still and let someone pour their blessing and adoration all over Him. He doesn't hold back on His gifts to people and He doesn't get in the way of others giving Him gifts.

With feasting we place our self-sufficiency on the altar. It is purposed. It is an act of faith to deliberately look to God to thank Him and revel in the beauty and care He graciously extends.

The purpose of fasting and feasting should never be obscured by the actual activity. In the coming week it is not necessary, nor is it healthy to starve yourself unwisely or stuff yourself mindlessly. As a matter of fact, there are many different parts of our lives that could be a fast as well as a feast. In one sense you starve your will to flood your life with God's call. In feasting you force yourself to bask in God's abundant grace instead of your own abilities. The first key is to master our appetite and our baser desires to better experience the fullness of the Spirit of God. The second key is to let yourself participate in a party you don't deserve.

DAY 36 · SON TESTED

 "As soon as Jesus was baptized, he went up out of the water. At that moment heaven was opened, and he saw the Spirit of God descending like a dove and alighting on him. And a voice from heaven said, "This is my Son, whom I love; with him I am well pleased." Then Jesus was led by the Spirit into the wilderness to be tempted by the devil. After fasting forty days and forty nights, he was hungry. The tempter came to him and said, "If you are the Son of God, tell these stones to become bread." (Matthew 3:16,17; 4:1-3)

 Temptation does not take hints well. Unless answered with a forceful "NO," followed by actions that support the statement, it will not back down until it has had its way.

The story is told of a boy's serious preparation for a time of temptation.

"Son," ordered a father, "Please don't swim in the canal."

"OK, Dad," he answered. But he came home carrying a wet bathing suit that evening.

"Where have you been?" demanded the father.

"Swimming in the canal," answered the boy. "Didn't I tell you not to swim there?" asked the father.

"Yes, Sir," answered the boy.

"Why did you?" he asked.

"Well, Dad," he explained, "I had my bathing suit with me and I couldn't resist the temptation."

"Why did you take your bathing suit with you?" he questioned.

"So I'd be prepared to swim, in case I was tempted," he replied.

So much for will power. This week the goal is to engage in the exercise of fasting for the purpose of strengthening our will power and opening up avenues to our heart and mind for God to speak through.

Fresh from the affirming voice of The Father announcing, "This is My Son" Jesus makes His way to the desert and fast for forty days. While very little is known about the encounter between Christ and Satan during these days of fasting, a couple of important insights are obvious.

Jesus goes to prepare for His ministry and to give His life as a ransom. Nothing will be harder to do than to die for humanity. This season wasn't an invitation to fight with Satan, but a time of selfless training in the desert became an opportunity for Satan to attack Christ.

The point of attack is His identity. Every temptation begins with, "If you are the Son of God..." The accuser sought to undermine Jesus with doubt. Lucifer uses the same old tired approach in garden for Adam and Eve. And even later in the ministry of Christ we hear the religious leaders taunt Jesus saying, "If you are the Son of God, come down and save yourself." Clearly, the point was to save people by His sacrifice, not save His own skin. But again, it begins with identity. The same is true for us today. Search each temptation we face and it is an attempt to drive us from who we really are—Children of God.

But Christ in the desert emerged victoriously as being "Son Tested." The word for "pure" in the Bible means to be tried by the sun. It evokes the way heat and light expose the true nature of a substance. During the first century, hucksters and crooks would take broken sculptures, clay pots and other earthenware and piece them together with melted wax for glue. It was quick and dirty. They whitewashed the items and sold them in the market. When people would place the sculptures or pots on the back porch in the middle-eastern sun, they would simply fall apart before their owner's eyes. It became somewhat of a catchphrase that if something was pure, it was "sun-tested, or made without wax.

Instead of being sons and daughters of God we become self-absorbed. The selfishness we embrace initially feels like freedom, but the more we give in to our wants and wishes we surrender to a part of our humanity that will ultimately cripple us. But if we choose surrender to God's will, even though it pinches our lifestyle or crosses our personal plans, a new inclination emerges. A strength of will tied to who we are, not what we do. When we exercise our will to align with His a chorus resonates in our soul—we are children and we belong to the Father. He shapes our identity and His will shapes our lives.

In fasting we see how our life aims too low. One student shared with me in frustration, "I wish God would just show me His will for my life!" I'm not exactly sure what that would look like: my life this year, next year, ten years, the end story... I answered by saying, "I wish God would show me many things too, but if God were to show you His will for your life with unmistakable clarity, you wouldn't believe it. His vision for you is far greater than your own imagination can envision."

""No eye has seen, no ear has heard, no mind has conceived what God has prepared for those who love him" (1 Corinthians 2:9)

God's vision for your life is described as being "In Christ."

In Christ...

I am a child of God (Romans 8:14,15/Galatians 3:26/John 1:12)

I am a new creation in Christ (2 Corinthians 5:17)

I am an heir with the Father (Galatians 4:6,7/Romans 8:17)

I am reconciled to God (2 Corinthians 5:18-19)

I am God's workmanship (Ephesians 2:10)

I am a citizen of heaven (Ephesians 2:19/Philippians 3:20)

I am a member of Christ's body (1 Corinthians 12:27)

I am the temple of the Holy Spirit (1 Corinthians 3:16/1 Corinthians 6:19)

I am a friend of Christ (John 15:15)

I am the righteousness of God (Romans 6:18/2 Corinthians 5:21)

I am chosen (John 15:16)

I am covered and hidden in Christ (Ephesians 4:24/Colossians 3:3/Galatians 3:27)

I am salt and light (Matthew 5:13)

I am more than a conqueror though Christ (Romans 8:37)

I am an alien and a stranger to this world (1 Peter 2:11)

I am saved by grace (Ephesians 2:8)

Fasting helps you learn little by little to surrender your petty little trinkets for God's choice gifts. So here is the challenge: Start fasting by choosing something reasonably small. Pick an area of your life in which you want to exercise abstinence for a day or two. Share your choice with your partner or your small group and encourage each other with the exercise.

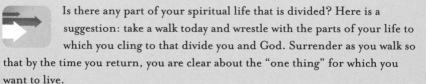

Is there any part of your spiritual life that is divided? Here is a suggestion: take a walk today and wrestle with the parts of your life to which you cling to that divide you and God. Surrender as you walk so that by the time you return, you are clear about the "one thing" for which you want to live.

Reflect on the things you have let go of throughout your life. Even from childhood. Consider all of the times you surrendered habits, feelings, and sins over to God so you could be free of them. Thank God for the process.

DAY 37 · "I" SURGERY

"And whenever you fast, do not look dismal, like the hypocrites, for they disfigure their faces so as to show others that they are fasting. Truly I tell you, they have received their reward. But when you fast, put oil on your head and wash your face, so that your fasting may be seen not by others but by your Father who is in secret; and your Father who sees in secret will reward you." (Matthew 6:16-18)

Since fasting targets the act of surrendering your appetite for something else to sustain you, Christ urges His followers to avoid making a show of it. In two separate places Jesus warns of this internal issue that shows up in conversations about "fasting." Furthermore, both examples are directed at people who are known to be "very spiritual."

EXAMPLE #1

You must understand how the Pharisees loved to be known as pure. Devoted. 100%. God's own true-blue, special-forces followers. What seemed to be at their heart was the desire to be seen as spiritual. People who fast are religious—very religious. Christ would say, "Be 'religious' but be subtle, otherwise your obvious religion outgrows and overshadows the God you serve." The ultimate end is that your will can become your god and many never see it coming. Since the core of fasting is to liberate us from our deep, sneaky loyalty to self, the visible effects are to be downplayed. Jesus said,

"Nothing outside a person can defile them by going into them. Rather, it is what comes out of a person that defiles them... For it is from within, out of a person's heart, that evil thoughts come—sexual immorality, theft, murder, adultery, greed, malice, deceit, lewdness, envy, slander, arrogance and folly. All these evils come from inside and defile a person." (Mark 7:15, 21-23)

EXAMPLE #2

If you think about the sins mentioned in this example you will notice that they begin inside with a hunger to put yourself first and not the act of putting self aside. Consider another example where Jesus takes on self and fasting:

To some who were confident of their own righteousness and looked down on everybody else, Jesus told this parable: "Two men went up to the temple to pray, one a Pharisee and the other a tax collector. The Pharisee stood up and prayed about himself: 'God, I thank you that I am not like other men—robbers, evildoers, adulterers—or even like this tax collector. I fast twice a week and give a tenth of all I get.' But the tax collector stood at a distance. He would not even look up to heaven, but beat his breast and said, 'God, have mercy on me, a sinner.' I tell you that this man, rather than the other, went home justified before God. For everyone who exalts himself will be humbled, and he who humbles himself will be exalted." (Luke 18:9-14)

In this parable, the Pharisee has got it all wrong. His view of God is wrong. His perception of himself is wrong. His pity for the publican is wrong. Anyone who points to God while pointing out their own piety is not only wrong but dangerously hard to help.

There are different types of sin. All sin is broken. All sin needs a Savior. But some sins seem to frustrate God's work in our life more than others. Self-sufficiency (I am enough), self-righteousness (I am good/right), and hypocrisy (I am known) are sins that God abhors because, by nature, they stiff-arm the hand of God reaching toward us. It is difficult for God to help us if we don't think we need help. Adultery, lying and stealing are bad, but those sins are beatable by the grace of God. What if you believe that you have no sin worth saving you from? Perhaps the most salient feature part of the problem is that people have an "I" disease but think they see clearly.

While walking in the downtown area of a major city, I clamored my way to stand in line at a cafe. Not looking where I was going I stepped on something and then heard a "yelp!" A dog was also waiting in line and I had stepped on its paw. The golden-haired dog was attached to a harness that was attached to the hand of a blind person. I felt horrible. "I stepped on the paw of a guide dog!" I chided myself quietly. I apologized to the woman and to the dog and then proceeded to converse with her while we waited to order. Jane was quick-witted and I enjoyed the warm banter that ensued after I offered to buy the assaulted dog (Roscoe) a doughnut.

"How long have you been unable to see?" I asked while we waited.

"Twenty five years. I was a teenager when I lost my sight." She replied. And then she added with a grin, "It's not so bad being blind. I get around. And as *you* know, even people who can see with their eyes fail to see where they are stepping." Ouch! She made the remark as philosophical as she could, but by the smile on her face betrayed her. She was referring to people like me, who can see quite well but will blindly step on a faithful dog's paw.

"Well said." I conceded as Jane and Roscoe went on their way.

The blind may not see with their eyes but they learn to trust other things to help them negotiate their way. It is those who are blind and think they see just fine that are hard to reach. In the parable above, Jesus exposes two kinds of blindness. Both men are sinners. The difference is that one swallows his pride while the other savors it as he swishes it around in his mouth. One sin can be cured, the other is terminal unless a massive tragedy occurs that breaks him down completely.

Jesus longs for us to surrender the self. He cheers when we practice, exercise, and challenge fasting against the appetites within us. Another way to say it is that Jesus wants us to put some distance between our wants and needs. What habit, activity, or behavior do you need to distance from your heart?

 Today, what activity do you need to distance yourself from for a day? Make a plan of how you will do this in such a way as not to draw attention to yourself.

Reflect on the experience of self-denial for the sake of renewal. How has this experience deepened your walk with God?

DAY 38 · AS FAST AS YOU CAN

"Now John's disciples and the Pharisees were fasting. Some people came and asked Jesus, "How is it that John's disciples and the disciples of the Pharisees are fasting, but yours are not?" Jesus answered, "How can the guests of the bridegroom fast while he is with them? They cannot, so long as they have him with them. But the time will come when the bridegroom will be taken from them, and on that day they will fast." (Mark 2:18-22)

Let's review. The reason to fast and "set something aside for a time" or "put something away" is to bridge the gap between your appetite and your actions. Another way to say it is to practice mastering the things you like in order that they don't master you. You never want to love something so much that you are unable to give it up.

There is nothing virtuous about denying yourself unless you are gaining separation from your wants to more consistently give yourself to needs. To strengthen your will to submit to God's is valuable. To distance yourself from activities to give God greater access to your heart, mind, and life is a priceless endeavor. Do it. Fast privately. Abstain joyfully. Surrender the little things so that you can remember who you are in reference to the big things.

Some put away sugar, TV, Facebook, ESPN, music, video games, coffee, feeling full, video games, etc... Others fast and put away the masks they hide behind, cheating to stay ahead or keep from getting behind, lying about their feelings, saying what you think no matter who it hurts, the relationships that are destructive, the anger they feel like they have a right to feel, and the unmistakable experience of being right. Still others will give up eating late, eating cheese, eating out, eating meat, or until they are full. One young man taught me to eat but leave the table a little hungry. Maybe there are many who do not feel shackled to bad habits, food or entertainment but give themselves to foolish causes. Perhaps the fast that God seeks is much broader in scope:

"Is not this the kind of fasting I have chosen:
to loose the chains of injustice
and untie the cords of the yoke,
to set the oppressed free
and break every yoke?
Is it not to share your food with the hungry
and to provide the poor wanderer with shelter—
when you see the naked, to clothe them,
and not to turn away from your own flesh and blood? (Isaiah 58:6,7)

Zell Kravinsky is a man who makes millions and literally spends it on others as fast as he is makes it. He is being both lauded and criticized by the public for the way he is gives his fortune away. His latest gift was a kidney for a woman he didn't even know. He had the tests completed and when he found he was a match for the woman, he left home early one morning without telling his wife and family, gave one of his kidneys to a complete stranger. We hear stories of people giving their organs to family members or even close friends, but to strangers? Some say he should have saved his kidney if perchance one of his own children should need it later on in life. Most people who know anything about Kravinsky are still not sure what to do with him. It is almost as if he is tuned into a different channel, so to speak. Maybe he is crazy. Maybe he is not so strapped to his money, or his own life.

Whether it be in the little things of life, like food or movies, or the big issues of justice and compassion, those who fast need to remember why they are doing it. It is possible to get into a rut where you do very few things you don't want to do and forget why? Consider this experiment that was conducted on monkeys:

"Four monkeys were placed in a room that had a tall pole in the center. Suspended from the top of that pole was a bunch of bananas. One of the hungry monkeys started climbing the pole to get something to eat, but just as he reached out to grab a banana, he was doused with a torrent of cold water. Squealing, he scampered away. Each monkey made a similar attempt, and each one was drenched with cold water. After making several attempts, they finally gave up.

The researchers removed one of the monkeys from the room and replaced him with a new monkey. As the newcomer began to climb the pole, the other three grabbed him and pulled him down to the ground. After trying to climb the pole several times and being dragged down by the others, he finally gave up and never attempted to climb the pole again.

The researchers replaced the original monkeys, one by one and each time a new monkey was brought in, he would be dragged down by the others before he could reach the bananas. In time, the room was filled with monkeys who had never received a cold shower. None of them would climb the pole, but none of them knew why."[3]

So it is with humanity. We can repeat good behaviors like fasting or praying or serving and not even know why. We can deny ourselves and exercise our will but lose sight of the purpose. When the disciples of John and the Pharisees broach the subject of fasting with Jesus they want to know why his own disciples don't fast as they do. There were required seasons of fasting in the era of Jesus, going all the way back to the Exodus. It was required to fast during some of the festivals, including Passover. But the Pharisees would also fast twice a week from 6 AM to 6 PM. Jesus answers with this cryptic, yet powerful image of and bridegroom and guests at a wedding.

In order to understand this response it is helpful to consider what a Hebrew wedding then would be like. The bride and the groom would not head out immediately for a honeymoon after the ceremony but would feast with their friends for a week in celebration. In a man's life, it was considered the most memorable time of his life. Feasting. Celebration. Joy. If fasting is to be an exercise Jesus urges His followers to engage in it should be no surprise that He is just as passionate about feasting.

 Reflect on what you have learned about your will, your appetite, and your needs in the few days we have been practicing fasting. Make a point to put on the calendar a day to fast and choose something to fast from that will deepen your joy in God's will and release you from the bonds of your own desires.

Prayer: "For those without food, grant bread; for those with bread, grant hunger for goodness, justice, and mercy."

DAY 39 · THE ONE THING—FIRST AND BEST

"As Jesus and his disciples were on their way, he came to a village where a woman named Martha opened her home to him. She had a sister called Mary, who sat at the Lord's feet listening to what he said. But Martha was distracted by all the preparations that had to be made. She came to him and asked, "Lord, don't you care that my sister has left me to do the work by myself? Tell her to help me!" "Martha, Martha," the Lord answered, "you are worried and upset about many things, but few things are needed—or indeed only one. Mary has chosen what is better, and it will not be taken away from her." (Luke 10:38-42)

A feast is…

Costly—it requires sharing my time, money and space.

Beautiful—it demands a well-set table, a clean house and tender care.

Intentional—there can be spontaneous gatherings but a feast takes planning.

Community—many must gather because anything less is self-centered.

Sensory—it invites calling forth our hearts and bodies along with our mind.

Feasting? Some might struggle to see extravagant celebrations or lavish meals as "discipline" or an "exercise" of the spiritual life. However, feasting is wired into our calendars (Christmas, Thanksgiving, Fourth of July, Birthdays, Weddings, Anniversaries, and even some funerals). Almost a quarter of the Jewish year was designated for some kind of feast. What is the nature and purpose of feasts for those who follow Jesus as His disciples?

As we conclude the Forty Days Wild with feasting it is with the understanding that you will be able to follow through on this subject without extra prompts.

Why feast? The answer is almost so simple we feel guilty calling it a reason: People. Love. Community. Hope. Forgiveness. Joy. Celebrate the amazing presence of those who God loves. Feast about the beauty and grace that comes from being capable of forgiveness. Dance. Eat. Sing. Laugh at the stories that portray our humanity and smile peacefully with a full stomach in the knowledge that people are created in the image of God.

The story of Martha and Mary inserts us as observers right in the crucial moments of a celebration. Martha is chopping onions, pots are boiling, bread is coming out of the oven, hundreds of things are happening in the kitchen and only two hands are doing the work. The feast is in the making but Martha complains that Mary is not pulling her weight to make the feast happen. For Martha, it's all about the meal. For Mary, it's all about the moment. Both are important, the meal and the moment, but Jesus declares that Mary has chosen the one thing everyone should choose: Him.

In order to feast, you must put everything else aside (in a similar way you fast by putting one thing away). Those who practice the discipline of feasting have jobs, medical visits, school bills, disobedient children, family members or friends in crisis, bad knees, migraines, messy houses, feelings of insecurity, memories of family members who have gone to sleep, people that annoy them, bosses that oppress them, lovers that ignore them and appliances that break and pipes that pop leaks at the most inconvenient times. But still you are called to celebrate—to feast.

Martha had her mind focused on "many things" but she needed a reminder about why they were gathered in the first place. Jesus was in their living room. He is the reason for the feast. He is not just their friend—He is the Son of God and He is sitting on their couch. Feasting is about stirring up love and all of its' effects through food and conversation.

The film, Babette's Feast, captures this sentiment perfectly. Set in 19th century Denmark, the film tells the story of a servant named Babette, who wins the lottery. With her newly acquired wealth she decides to spend her winnings hosting an extravagant feast for her two mean-spirited bosses and all their friends. All the guests are on the older side of life and they all have what we would call "baggage." The two sisters (bosses) grew up as the daughters of a former pastor and have lived all their lives scared to enjoy the pleasures of this world.

Two other guests that attend used to be old friends but got in a fight years ago and stopped speaking to each other. Another guest is an older man who never confessed his love for a certain woman. And so on.

In the movie the guests willingly attend but vow not to speak a word about the meal or the gathering. The guests are so set in their misery they resolve to endure the occasion with glum resignation. The feast blows them away. Babette's meal is beyond anything they had ever imagined, and the guests get lost in the beauty and spirit of the moment. Her lottery winnings afforded rare delicacies, rich and unimagined dishes never seen or tasted in that little town. Course after course, the heavenly banquet breaks down their fearful dispositions and petty hatred. By the end the guests all swept up by the beauty of Babette's generosity. The feast creates an atmosphere where forgiveness, love and joy wash over the people and everyone is changed.

Food is a large part of Babette's magic, but it's not all. The movie implies something far more spiritual is at work as well. In Bethany the food is important, as Martha would attest, but the magic has to do with what Mary embraced she paid attention to Christ.

So, plan a feast. Plan it well. Plan for the people that gather. Celebrations are not about events, but about eventful people. Feasts are not about special occasions on a calendar, but the people who make moments matter.

 Plan a meal with friends with the purpose showing the people how important they are. Divide up the roles and the responsibilities, but convey the standard that excellence and abundance are the goal. Plan a feast to simply celebrate the people in your life. Consider inviting people along a spectrum of how well you know them.

DAY 40 · WE HAD TO CELEBRATE

"But the father said to his servants, 'Quick! Bring the best robe and put it on him. Put a ring on his finger and sandals on his feet. Bring the fattened calf and kill it. Let's have a feast and celebrate. For this son of mine was dead and is alive again; he was lost and is found.' So they began to celebrate.

"Meanwhile, the older son was in the field. When he came near the house, he heard music and dancing. So he called one of the servants and asked him what was going on. 'Your brother has come,' he replied, 'and your father has killed the fattened calf because he has him back safe and sound.'

"The older brother became angry and refused to go in. So his father went out and pleaded with him. But he answered his father, 'Look! All these years I've been slaving for you and never disobeyed your orders. Yet you never gave me even a young goat so I could celebrate with my friends. But when this son of yours who has squandered your property with prostitutes comes home, you kill the fattened calf for him!'

"'My son,' the father said, 'you are always with me, and everything I have is yours. But we had to celebrate and be glad, because this brother of yours was dead and is alive again; he was lost and is found.'" (Luke 15:1-32)

The significance of the phrase, "There is more joy in heaven…" cannot be overstated when you read Luke 15.

The Lost Sheep. The Lost Coin. The Prodigal Son. All three stories seem to have their own identity and can be told separately. Even the "Prodigal Son" story is most often told without mention of the older brother. Occasionally some will refer to the behavior of the older brother as an afterthought or final warning, but the central purpose of all these stories centers in the response of the older brother to the feast.

Notice why this parable is told: "Now the tax collectors and "sinners" were all gathering around to hear him. But the Pharisees and the teachers of the law muttered, "This man welcomes sinners and eats with them." (Luke 15:1,2) In middle-eastern culture nothing is more sacred to a community than eating a meal with someone. Anyone who travels through the lands will speak of the profound hospitality that permeates the place. The fact that Jesus "welcomes" and "eats with them" speaks to the degree that he bonded with those that would be considered, "sinners." So, this parable is an answer to the complaint of the Pharisees and teachers of the law (The older brother).

So wherever the story takes us—they must land a response to the reality that Jesus bound himself to sinners.

The Sheep is found. Heaven rejoices. The coin is recovered. Heaven celebrates. The younger son severs his relationship to the father, leaves the family in shame only to return when he runs out of options. If you asked people who live in that part of the world if a father would ever, 1) be watching, 2) run to meet the boy, 3) count him as a son after the way he disowned the family, 4) consider him a son and throw a feast, most people there would shake their head and say: Impossible.

But the father put s the best robe on his filthy prodigal, places a ring on his finger and throws a feast to celebrate HIS JOY that HIS SON is alive and home.

When the older brother hears the noise of a party he, "Refused to go in." In that culture it was the older brother's responsibility to show hospitality to all the guests. His refusal to participate would be a slap to the face of the father and the rest of the family. But in the same way that the father runs down the road to meet the younger prodigal, he goes out to the courtyard to plead with the older son. Notice the exchange:

"So his father went out and pleaded with him. But he answered his father, 'Look! All these years I've been slaving for you and never disobeyed your orders." (Luke 15:29)

As far as the older brother is concerned, the relationship between him and his father is gone. He doesn't use the respectful term "O Father" nor does he seize upon the truth that he is his eldest son. The younger son left, but the older son stayed. But the older son does not consider himself a son—but a servant. He didn't stay for love, but for obedience. He doesn't define value by relationship, but he clings to his rights. The younger brother was selfish but the older brother is self-righteous. One son broke the Father's heart and left. The other son broke the Father's heart even though he obeyed and stayed. The bottom line is that He, "refused to go in" to the feast. The younger son had nowhere else to go. He is probably sitting there quietly stunned that he is a son, again.

The father pleads with the older son saying, "My son,' the father said, 'you are always with me, and everything I have is yours. But we had to celebrate and be glad…" The father couldn't help himself. The party isn't for the younger son it is for the Father who can't help but to feast. As we wind up the *Forty Days Wild* we conclude with an invitation to the feast. The Father has to celebrate! Grace has come and restored those who are lost. We must feast! Why? Because something— Someone greater than our sin has covered our shame. We must sing, dance, eat, and shout with joy! This is the biggest, most important thing that has ever happened.

The parable is the only one I know that is not finished. The Father and son are left in the courtyard with the father making a plea and inviting the older son to come in to the feast and celebrate. A feast isn't about what is fair it is about abundance grace, which produces irrepressible joy. There is a no fair amount of joy.

Such glimpses of salvation and feasting must occur in our homes and churches today.

I'd like to make a challenge that anytime someone returns to God and finds this good news of salvation, there must be a feast. A loud, abundant, well-prepared, grace-filled banquet that declares on earth what is going on in heaven.

 Plan a feast for your friends, family or local community of faith that celebrates the day they came to Christ. Plan a feast to celebrate God's saving work in your life. Call it a Joyous Father party. Invite people to tell their stories. Sing favorite songs. Above all, remember to bring an abundance of food to mirror the amazing grace of God. Reflect on the coming day when God will feast with us in heaven.

Revelation 19:7
"Let us rejoice and be glad and give him glory!
For the wedding of the Lamb has come,
and his bride has made herself ready."

Revelation 21:2
"I saw the Holy City, the new Jerusalem,
coming down out of heaven from God,
prepared as a bride beautifully dressed for her husband."

Revelation 22:17
"The Spirit and the bride say, "Come!"
And let him who hears say, "Come!"
Whoever is thirsty, let him come; and whoever wishes,
let him take the free gift of the water of life."

[1] Dallas Willard, The Spirit of the Disciplines, (New York: Harper Collins, 1988), p. 172.

[2] Ibid, p. 166.

[3] John C. Maxwell, Failing Forward, (Nashville, Tennessee: Thomas Nelson, 2000), p.47, 48.

Who do you know that seems to be able to "do God's will" even if the challenges they face are undesirable? How do they do it?

What are some uncertain areas of your life you want to trust God with this week?

What do you think are the pitfalls of fasting?
How would you describe the benefits?

What are some creative approaches to fasting that you found helpful?

Of the three sins mentioned this week (self sufficiency, self-righteousness, hypocrisy), which tends to live in you more than you would like? What kind of fast will enable you to be more like the publican referred to this week?

In what area(s) of your life do you long to be more single-minded about?

How does the disciplines of fasting and feasting complicate your life?
How is it liberating?

What are some goals/ideas you have about incorporating the disciplines of fasting and feasting in your life?

What do you think about the prayer of the publican? In what way is the prayer of the publican easy to pray, how might it be difficult?